# MISSOURI-KANSAS-TEXAS LINES

## In Color

By Raymond B. George, Jr.

Published by
**Morning Sun Books, Inc.**
11 Sussex Court
Edison, N.J. 08820
Library of Congress Catalog Card Number: 93-080947
Typesetting and layout by R.B. George, Jr., with
assistance from R.J. Yanosey of Morning Sun Books

First Printing
ISBN 1-878887-28-9

*Dedicated to my wife Lynn, in celebration of our twenty years together.*

# ACKNOWLEDGEMENTS

*B*ringing together this collection of rare and historic photographs would have been impossible without the help of many people who share a common vision. Credit for the original idea for an all color Katy book goes to publisher Bob Yanosey, who was also this book's proofreader. In addition, special attention must be given to Earl Holloway, who recommended this writer's name to Bob Yanosey of Morning Sun as the possible author. As soon as work began, Earl Holloway was the first contributor for this volume and entrusted his entire collection of almost two thousand MKT color transparencies to the author for a period of over one year.

Bob Yanosey's reputation as a publisher who gets projects completed on time earned him the respect of Emery J. Gulash, who is the chief contributor of steam-era coverage in this book. To Emery's credit, his color photographs of MKT steam power are the finest that have ever been published.

While in the planning stages, the author realized a book about the Katy would be incomplete without contributions from John B. Charles and the slides taken by Arthur G. Charles, John's late father. The combined efforts of father and son, who were both employees of the Katy Railroad, form the largest portion of this book's photographs.

We are fortunate William J. Neill's fondness for his former boss, the late R.B. George (MKT's Vice President of Operations in the 1960's), was a key factor in the decision to send his collection of Katy slides to this writer for consideration. As with this incident, the influence of the author's late father, R.B. George, Sr., has touched each page of this volume in some manner.

Other contributors, most of whom are members of the Katy Railroad Historical Society, were Mike and Steven Bledsoe, C.A. Snarrenberg, the author's late sister Mary Lee Forderhase, Dr. Tom Hughes, Timothy Brickner, L.W. Jacobs, Jr., the late Howard Killam, Frank Watson, Michael Warden Thomas, Al Chione, Helen Chester and her late husband Ellis Chester, the late Roy Rude, Robert T. Fillman, the late R.S. Plummer, Don M. Christisen, S.M. Ploeger, Dr. Theron Baber, Thomas R. Lee, Walter E. Zullig, Jr., Mel Nierdieck, B. Allen Young, Dr. Louis A. Marre, J.O.B. Johnson, C.F. Webb, Bruce Blalock, Tom Balzen, Craig Shaw, Charles D. Hunter, Scott Muskopf, David Fasules, Jim Hurt and the late Fred Lyon, founder of the K.R.H.S.

Assistance with research on Katy rolling stock and locomotives came from Jerry Pitts, Harry R. Brown, Gary Bagby, Harry Sweet, James Hellums and Martin F. Rister. Jim Bantin of the Western Historical Manuscript Collection at the University of Missouri-Columbia patiently helped the author with steam locomotive disposition records in the Fred Lyon Collection.

America's greatest railroad artist, Howard Fogg, generously talked to the author about his experiences with the Katy Railroad and also allowed the use of one of his excellent early watercolor paintings in this volume.

Lastly, Joe G. Collias, the author's longtime friend and fellow St. Louisan, was an important advisor on this project. Joe's numerous railroad books were a constant source of inspiration, including *Katy Power*, co-authored with this writer in 1986. Joe Collias' high standards will always be the mark to shoot for.

# MISSOURI-KANSAS-TEXAS LINES
## In Color

The Missouri-Kansas-Texas (Katy) Railroad ceased operations as an independent corporation on August 11, 1988, ending a span of 118 years of continuous service to the central and southwestern United States. Although labeled as a "regional carrier," the Katy became well known throughout the country by means of favorable publicity in national rail publications and periodicals starting in the 1920's and 30's. It was a small rail system when compared to the likes of a New York Central or Union Pacific; however, the MKT was operated with a great sense of efficiency and pride that overcame almost any difficulty. These traits were a reflection of top management, which carefully nurtured a "family" atmosphere among employees and the public, until a change in management philosophy came to the Katy in 1957. This change assured the Katy's survival for an additional 30 years, but drastically altered the physical appearance of the road and its operating methods. Much of what Katy did between 1957 and 1965 to avoid bankruptcy has become standard practice among the surviving giant rail systems of the 1990's. Though it seems unfortunate to many, Katy's sale to Union Pacific in 1988 by parent Katy Industries Corporation was the fulfillment of top management's longtime goal of finding a suitable marriage partner for "Miss Katy."

This volume is intended to briefly show the Katy at its best, in beautiful color, during the height of its steam and early diesel years, through difficult times in the late 1950's, into the dramatic rebuilding period of the 1960's and 70's, leading to the unparalleled success of the 1980's. In addition to excellent color photography, covering the period 1943-1988, a brief history is appropriate because the MKT was a pioneer road of the Southwest and much of Katy's "charm" comes from her past.

Ironically, the Katy was originally chartered as the Union Pacific Railway, Southern Branch in 1865; ground was broken October 15, 1867 at Junction City, Kansas. The railroad's name officially changed to the Missouri, Kansas & Texas Railway by a resolution dated March 31, 1870. The sometimes confusing omission of the word "Oklahoma" from the corporate name and emblem came about because that future state was still the Indian Territory in 1870 when the line was conceived.

The origin of the famous nickname "Katy" has been traced to 1880, when the M.K.&T. entered an eight year period of control by Jay Gould's Missouri Pacific Railroad. In that year the M.K.&T. was advertised as the "Kansas & Texas Division" of the Missouri Pacific Railroad in printed public timetables and newspapers. Railroad employees and the public shortened this to the endearing KT, or "Katy."

The M.K.&T.'s early developers were interested in obtaining government land grants in southeastern Kansas and building the first railroad to Texas through the Indian Territory. The winning of a frantic construction race to the Cherokee lands of the Indian Territory in 1870 gained a valuable land grant and the necessary construction rights. Completion of the Indian Territory line came with the crossing of the Red River Bridge and arrival of the first regular train at the new town of Denison, Texas on Christmas day 1872. Denison later became operating headquarters of the Katy system.

The generous Indian Territory land grant, totalling 3,110,400 acres, was eventually lost by the Katy in 1914 when the Supreme Court upheld a lower court decision that stripped the railroad of its enormous holdings, except for a right-of-way 200 feet wide and the land for necessary shops and yards. This earned for Katy the reputation of being a "Hard Luck" road that struggled for its survival totally on its own, unlike the land grant giants it competed with.

Like Denison, numerous cities along the line owe their existence to the M.K.&T., including Parsons, Kansas, which was established as the operating hub of the early system in 1870; it was named in honor of the Katy's first president, Judge Levi Parsons. An eastern division between Parsons and Sedalia, Missouri was completed in 1871 that gave the M.K.& T. access to St. Louis, Missouri, through interchange with its arch rival, the Missouri Pacific Railraod. A limited connection to Chicago was obtained with the completion of a line between Sedalia and Hannibal, Missouri in 1873 and the establishment of interchange agreements with the Chicago, Burlington & Quincy.

Expansion of the M.K.&T. system in the state of Texas began during Jay Gould's control from 1880 to 1888. Entry into Dallas and Ft. Worth came in 1881 and another route to Dallas via Greenville, Texas was completed in 1886. Portions of lines to both San Antonio and Houston were surveyed or underway before the M.K.&T. was ordered to be operated separately from the Missouri Pacific by the courts in 1888. The Katy entered San Antonio on its own rails in 1901, but completed a more direct route there via Austin,

San Antonio/Houston. As St. Louis developed into the primary gateway to the East, the Hannibal line declined in importance; the Moberly-Hannibal section was eventually leased in 1923, and later sold, to the Wabash Railroad.

Remaining line construction or route acquisition centered on feeder lines to the main Katy system. The larger additions were the Texas Central Railroad, from Waco to Rotan, Texas in 1910; the Wichita Falls & Northwestern system, from Wichita Falls, Texas, to Forgan, Oklahoma, in 1911; construction of the Tulsa Division between Muskogee and Osage, Oklahoma, in 1903; and completion of a line from Parsons, Kansas to Oklahoma City, in 1904.

In 1943 the Katy operated and maintained a total of 3,293 miles of track in four states. The only mainline double track on the system was a 52 mile section between Stringtown, Oklahoma and the Red River bridge into Texas. Branch line steel was as light as 66-pound, with the majority of mainline laid with 90-pound rail. Katy's executive

*(Left)* In 1889 the Katy approved the design for a corporate emblem submitted by the Rand McNally Company that served the railroad well, until its demise in 1988. Inside the emblem were the road's initials and a ribbon with the full corporate name. Behind the ribbon were palm leaves symbolizing victory in the 1870 Indian Territory race. The ribbon signifies the Katy's arrival in Texas in 1872 as the first railroad from the north. Rounded shapes at the top and bottom of the herald are reminiscent of Spanish architectural design elements, similar to the pediment of San Antonio's famous Alamo; quite fitting for this southwestern pioneer. Every Katy president, with the exception of William Deramus, III, used this herald as the railroad's symbol from 1889 to 1988, with only slight modifications. *(Steven Bledsoe)*

Texas in 1905. The line to Houston was laid in 1893 and direct access to the port of Galveston was obtained through joint ownership of the Galveston, Houston and Henderson Railroad. A route between Denison and Wichita Falls, Texas was completed in 1895.

Construction and acquisition of lines in Kansas in the 1880's brought the Katy to the outskirts of Kansas City, which was reached in 1889 through a trackage rights agreement. In 1893 the Katy's own line to St. Louis was finished along the north bank of the Missouri River and the road's first named train, THE KATY FLYER, began service between St. Louis/Kansas City and

headquarters were located in St. Louis and New York City, with other major offices at Dallas, Texas and Parsons, Kansas. Train dispatching was handled by six sparate offices.

By 1988 3,377 miles of track was operated in six midwestern states by the MKT and its subsidiary, the Oklahoma, Kansas and Texas Railroad. Welded rail of 115 and 133-pounds was the standard on the Houston–Kansas City corridor. Executive offices were at Dallas, with operating and accounting departments headquartered at Denison. Dispatching for the MKT / OKT system was centered at Denison, with locomotive maintenance performed at the Parsons, Kansas shops.

The Katy was fortunate to have been led by an outstanding group of chief executives during its last 75 years, starting with Charles E. Schaff in 1912. Mr. Schaff is credited with acquiring Katy's largest classes of steam freight and passenger power, which necessitated upgrading the entire physical plant of the road between 1913 and 1923. Through an eight year receivership and corporate reorganization, Mr. Schaff spent more than $50 million on improvements and new facilities, including the construction of many of the most attractive station buildings. Among the results of the reorganization was a change in the corporate name to the Missouri-Kansas-Texas Railroad Co., with the deletion of the "&" between Kansas and Texas. Improvements continued after Mr. Schaff's retirement in 1926, until the Wall Street Crash of 1929 forced two unlucky successors, Columbus Haile and M.H. Cahill, into early retirement.

The company was nearing bankruptcy in 1934 when Matthew S. Sloan was asked by the Board of Directors to take charge of the road's operations. Mr. Sloan's background was entirely in engineering and public utilities, having been with the New York Edison Company from 1917 to 1932, when he resigned as its president to join the Katy's executive committee. No previous Katy president personally supervised the road's operation as did Mr. Sloan, who could turn up at any location on the railroad at almost any time. When not in Katy business car No. 400 on the rails between St. Louis and New York City,

where his office and home were maintained, Mr. Sloan was on inspection tours of the MKT in his chauffeur driven 1936 Chrysler *Airflow* sedan that was painted bright yellow, equipped with flanged wheels and fender mounted seats. With operating revenues at a virtual standstill during the seven year period prior to World War II, Mr. Sloan's personal involvement proved a key factor in the Katy's survival. His passion for neatness became renowned, as was the use of his favorite color in paint for Katy structures and rolling stock (probably influenced by his career in the utility field), known far and wide as "Sloan Yellow."

Through the suspension of dividends on Katy common stock and 7% preferred cumulative stock, starting in 1932, Mr. Sloan was able to maintain the railroad and make limited improvements only on an "as-needed" basis during the depressed years of the 1930's. Loans were received from the Reconstruction Finance Corporation in 1935 and 1938 that narrowly kept the Katy from the court's control.

Famine turned to feast during the war years 1941-1945, with gross revenues rising to $84 million in 1944. Oil traffic alone accounted for as many as 14 extra tank trains per day during the height of the war, not to mention extra military movements, or "Main Trains." Locomotive bad orders were reportedly reduced to a respectable 7% of the fleet. Mr. Sloan spent over $100 million on necessary expenditures and an additional $40 million toward the retirement of company mortgage bonds before his untimely death on June 14, 1945.

*(Above)* Designed by New York architect Frederick J. Sterner, the San Antonio, Texas passenger station was the most handsome structure on the entire Katy system. This was the southern terminal for M-K-T's KATY FLYER, ALAMO SPECIAL, BLUEBONNET and premier TEXAS SPECIAL. Formal ceremonies opened the facility on September 1, 1917. No. 1, the TEXAS SPECIAL, was the last passenger train to arrive at the station on July 26, 1964. In 1968 this unique building was demolished because it was considered a tax liability. *(C.A. Snarrenberg)*

The hard driving Matt Sloan was followed by Raymond J. Morfa as Katy's Board Chairman on October 1, 1945. Mr. Morfa came to the Katy with a reputation for getting things done and had formerly been with the Chesapeake & Ohio and Nickel Plate roads.

Mr. Morfa's most formidable task was the complete dieselization of Katy motive power, which had been delayed by Mr. Sloan because of the war; a postwar economic boom in the Southwest facilitated this effort. In addition to diselization, the Katy became a pioneer in the use of two-way radios in yard use and on regular service through freights. Agreements were signed with the Frisco Railroad to initiate the first all-streamlined diesel powered train in regular service between Texas and St. Louis. An able morale builder, Mr. Morfa began a system wide program of promotions from within the Katy's own ranks, starting with the elevation of Donald V. Fraser from the position of executive assistant to the post of president on October 23, 1945. The Morfa/Fraser administration, from 1945 to 1952, is considered to be one of the most colorful and progressive eras of the road's long history. Up to the close of the Korean conflict in 1953, annual gross revenues remained at or near their World War II levels. This permitted the M-K-T to proudly maintain its dwindling number of steam locomotives in sparkling condition until all, save one, were removed from service and scrapped. Mr. Morfa's sudden death on October 19, 1952 shocked the entire Katy family.

President Donald V. Fraser accepted the additional duties of Board Chairman in November 1952 and set about grappling with Katy's enormous debt load, as well as reducing unnecessary expenditures. In 1952 the M-K-T still employed over 10,000 workers, roughly the same number employed during the labor intensive postwar days of steam. Mr. Fraser quietly reduced that number to 7,500 by 1956, through attrition and retirements. The Katy's Sedalia, Missouri passenger car shops were closed in 1956, in addition to several branch line abandonments. Consolidations of passenger routes and dispatching centers were made, along with the establishment of a subsidiary trucking line, with Interstate Commerce Commission approval.

Unfortunately, Mr. Fraser failed to gain ICC approval for recapitalization plans submitted in 1952 and 1955 that could have dealt with a massive debt caused by the suspension of preferred stock dividends during the Depression; by 1956 over $100 million in unpaid dividends had accumulated. Gross income dropped from $85 million in 1953 to $72 million in 1954 and could not be appreciably increased in 1955 and 1956, due to a protracted drought in the southwest and a general decline in business and military activities. A serious illness temporarily affected Mr. Fraser in April 1956 that caused the executive committee to bring William N. Deramus, III to the Katy as its president on January 8, 1957. Mr. Fraser stayed on as Chairman of the Board, until retirement from active duty at his own request on May 5, 1961.

*(Left)* Katy's one surviving steam locomotive is an exquisite little 4-4-0 American Type, #311. It is pictured as it was in 1952, camouflaged as an 1870's antique for celebrations at Parsons, Kansas and Denison, Texas. Katy then donated the engine and several early cars to the National Museum of Transportation in St. Louis on September 25, 1952. Originally numbered 200 when built by Baldwin in 1890, it was later renumbered 311 and rebuilt in the Parsons shops in 1923 with a new boiler and superheater. Superheaters were a necessary improvement to Katy 4-4-0s to increase operating efficiency for passenger service on various branch lines in the 1930's and 40's. No. 311 was fully capable of speeds in excess of 60 miles per hour and represents the highest state of evolution of the American Type. *(Mary Lee Forderhase)*

William N. Deramus, III had been president of the Chicago Great Western Railroad since 1948; his family also held controlling interest in the Kansas City Southern Railroad. Because so much of Katy's resources serviced its enormous debt load, its physical plant had declined in the mid-1950's. This, coupled with an alarming jump in bad order locomotives from 4% in 1956 to 35% in 1958, became justification for major changes. Mr. Deramus was given authority from the executive committee to make drastic revisions that were essential for the road's survival. Every part of Katy operations was closely scrutinized by Deramus and his lieutenants to determine if they were of value to the company. Unprofitable branch lines and passenger routes were the obvious items to be eliminated, followed by station closings and reduction of the work force; the number of employees was eventually cut to 3,000 by 1959 and remained at that level for the next three decades.

President Deramus firmly believed longer trains was the most efficient way to operate a railroad and instigated the use of up to eight diesel units pulling 200 car freight drags. Some trains were held at terminals until a sufficient number of cars had been assembled before Mr. Deramus personally gave permission for their departure. Because of the motive power shortage, due to bad orders, power was leased from the Wabash, Chicago Great Western, Kansas City Southern and even the Pennsylvania. At least one mighty Baldwin Centipede saw service on the hills between Franklin, Missouri and Parsons, Kansas before it was returned to the Pennsy. Customer service declined during this period, with gross revenues from car loadings showing a drop each year from 1956 to 1963.

Construction of the U.S. interstate highway system in the Midwest during the late 1950's heralded a steady fall in passenger ridership on the Katy Lines. With ICC approval, Deramus eliminated unprofitable KATY FLYER service to St. Louis over Katy's own route in 1958 and terminated the contract with the Frisco Railroad for the joint operation of the TEXAS SPECIAL on January 4, 1959. Katy's BLUEBONNET ceased operation between Kansas City and Houston on that date also. Eventually, all Katy passenger service ended on June 30, 1965, due primarily to the continued loss of U.S. mail contracts to the bids of highly competitive trucking firms.

To Mr. Deramus' credit, the ICC approved a corporate recapitalization plan in 1958 that finally dealt with Katy's heavy debt obligations. New technology was introduced to the Katy in the form of a computerized accounting system and the expanded use of two-way radio communications. Katy motive power was completely revitalized during the Deramus years through simplification and standardization. Costly parts inventories were reduced by rebuilding the roadswitcher fleet with GM's Electro-Motive Division prime movers and the retirement or resale of most of Katy's passenger power. Large expenditures were made toward track maintenance and yard modernization in 1957-58, but could not be sustained due to declining revenues. After four tumultuous years as Katy's president, Mr. Deramus resigned in 1961 to succeed his ailing father as president of the Kansas City Southern.

*(Right)* Among the most drastic symbolic changes authorized by Mr. Deramus was the redesign of the Katy's famous emblem. The new herald is on engine #131 at Durant, Oklahoma on October 2, 1963. Like the emblem, Katy's motive power was also simplified and revised. No. 131 was built by Baldwin in 1950 as an AS-16 and numbered 1576, then rebuilt with a 1500 HP EMD prime mover in 1960, renumbered 131 and repainted red with black chassis and running gear. The new paint scheme was stark, yet recognizable and, most importantly, easily maintained. *(Earl Holloway)*

*(Left)* There was no mistaking which railroad's facility this was, due to an encore of company emblems. New EMD GP-40 #197 and F-3 #64C were found in the Katy's Sloan Yard at San Antonio, Texas in August, 1969. No. 197 was among a group of seventy-one new locomotives acquired during John Barriger's presidency from 1965 to 1970. One of the first steps taken by Mr. Barriger, upon coming to the Katy, was the restoration of the original herald, the only change being the replacement of the initials M-K-T with the more popular "KATY."
*(Dr. Tom Hughes)*

Charles T. Williams, former Katy vice president of operations, was selected to replace Mr. Deramus by the Board of Directors on November 1, 1961. Like Mr. Fraser before him, Mr. Williams spent his entire career on the Katy and had risen through the ranks. C.T. Williams is well remembered as a talented and efficient division level superintendent, but this did not prepare him for the enormous executive task of saving the Katy. Although substantial loans were acquired in 1961, Williams intensified the program of drastic curtailment of service and maintenance. By the end of 1964, the Katy had reached the brink of financial and physical collapse and its bankruptcy was predicted by industry analysts. Under these circumstances John Walker Barriger, III, was elected Chairman of the Board on March 11, 1965 and exchanged that post for the presidency in May, 1965.

Mr. Barriger was perhaps his generation's greatest railroader, having begun his career as a student trainee on the Pennsylvania Railroad in 1917. From 1933 to 1941 he was chief of the Railroad Division of the U.S. Reconstruction Finance Corporation, in charge of $1½ billion. In that capacity he had initially refused the M-K-T's appeal for assistance during the Depression. He believed correctly that it would have been better for the Katy to have reorganized and been declared bankrupt in the 1930's, rather than struggle along with deferred maintenance and development that placed it under competitive handicaps in following years. Barriger had also been president of the Monon Railroad and the

wealthy Pittsburgh & Lake Erie Railroad, in addition to holding executive posts on many other roads. Lucius Beebe once referred to him as, "The Last of the Great Magnificos."

Mr. Barriger was a master of public relations, and immediately began a personal survey of the railroad, explaining Katy's problems and seeking the cooperation of communities, shippers and employees through speeches and newspaper interviews. Bulldozed wrecks along the right-of-way were cleaned up and other scrap accounted for $1 million in salvage. Mr. Barriger added switch engines and a second St. Louis train, insisting, "Service is the only thing a railroad has to sell!" To facilitate the acquisition of financing in 1967, he supported the creation of Katy Industries Corporation, a diversified parent company of the M-K-T Railroad. Mr. Barriger's ultimate plan was to effect Katy's merger with one of the great rail systems of the West.

Track was rehabilitated and over 3,000 new freight cars and 70 new locomotives were in sevice by 1969. Mr. Barriger brought national attention to the Katy through his inspiring efforts and received several prestigious industry awards; not the least of these was being named "Railroad Man Of The Year" in January 1969 by *Modern Railroads* magazine. With the exception of finding the perfect merger partner, most of his goals for the Katy had been met by 1970, the year of Mr. Barriger's retirement at age 70. Since Mr. Barriger's death in 1976, the U.S. railroading scene has not been the same.

Reginald N. Whitman became Katy's President and Chief Operating Officer on July 15, 1970. As a Federal Railroad Administration executive and President of the government-owned Alaska Railroad, Mr. Whitman had previously gained a unique understanding of government's relationship with U.S. railroads.

Forty years of deferred track maintenance, performed on an "as needed" basis, had left Katy trackage in generally mediocre condition. In 1974 this policy changed when the Lower Colorado River Authority came to the Katy with a proposition requiring the frequent transport of coal trains between Ft. Worth and a new power plant on the Houston Subdivision near LaGrange, Texas. The proposal was contingent upon Katy's ability to upgrade 245 miles of mainline to the highest standards. To this end, Mr. Whitman supervised the acquisition of federally guaranteed loans totalling $19 million in 1975. Heavier 115 pound rail was laid and up to 2,000 ties to the mile inserted between Houston and Ft. Worth. Katy expenditures totalled $400 million for system improvements by 1981, resulting in additional traffic and a second power plant location at Pryor, Oklahoma. During this period, gross revenues increased from $76 million in 1971 to $273 million in 1981. Mr. Whitman gives credit for this dramatic success to Katy's dedicated employees and a modicum of "Good Luck." On January 1, 1979, Mr. Whitman was elected Chairman of the Board and continued working closely with Harold L. Gastler, Katy's new President. Mr. Gastler was previously with the Frisco Railroad and had been Katy's Vice President of Operations during the 70's.

In 1980-82 the Whitman/Gastler administration negotiated with the trustee of the bankrupt Rock Island Railroad, the state of Oklahoma and a shippers association to acquire or operate most of the Rock's Kansas, Oklahoma and Texas routes. A new Katy subsidiary was created in 1980, named the Oklahoma, Kansas and Texas Railroad, that operated 630 miles of line between Salina, Kansas and the Dallas/Ft. Worth metroplex. The OKT registered healthy profits in 1987 and 1988, due to the good export grain market at that time.

Katy's legal protest against the Union Pacific/Missouri Pacific merger in 1981 resulted in the acquisition of trackage rights on the Union Pacific's Omaha Subdivision and in Kansas. The Union Pacific and Katy eventually shared over 600 miles of trackage rights by the spring of 1985, when the first plan for UP's purchase of the Katy was announced. A trade-off agreement with the Union Pacific in 1986 gave the Katy operating rights on the UP between Sedalia and St. Louis, Missouri, while UP gained rights on Katy's central Oklahoma corridor. This agreement permitted the Katy to dispose of its own line to St. Louis in 1987. Legal details and ICC approval delayed the UP's takeover until August 11, 1988, the last day of independent Katy operations. Union Pacific purchased the Katy system for $110 million and assumed MKT's $250 million debt.

Little remains today to remind us of the Katy Railroad, due to the UP's quick retirement or repainting of MKT rolling stock and the consolidation of facilities. The following record of achievement will hopefully be a tribute to this courageous road.

*(Right)* Katy locomotives were painted a distinctive green with yellow stripes during the Whitman/Gastler years. Between 1978 and 1981, 37 new 3,000 HP EMD SD40-2s, numbered 600 to 636, were purchased, becoming Katy's heaviest power. Originally, these engines were acquired for coal hauling service and were seldom seen north of Ft. Worth, Texas. By 1988, improved track conditions permitted their use systemwide, except on branch lines and the St. Louis route. *(Timothy Brickner)*

# MISSOURI-KANSAS-TEXAS RAILROAD
## MOTIVE POWER, 1943 - 1988

### STEAM POWER SUMMARY, AS OF DECEMBER 31, 1943

| WHEEL ARRANGEMENT | TYPE | SERIES NUMBER | QUANTITY |
|---|---|---|---|
| 0-4-0 | 4 WHEEL SWITCHER | 92 - 93 | 2 |
| 0-6-0 | 6 WHEEL SWITCHER | 5 - 37 | 23 |
| 0-8-0 | 8 WHEEL SWITCHER | 39 - 68, 101 - 110 | 40 |
| 4-4-0 | AMERICAN | 306 - 315 | 6 |
| 4-6-2 | PACIFIC | 350 - 412 | 59 |
| 2-6-0 | MOGUL | 476 - 596 | 35 |
| 2-8-0 | CONSOLIDATION | 608 - 670 | 17 |
| 2-8-2 | MIKADO | 702 - 920 | 130 |
| - | RAIL MOTOR CAR | M-10 - M-12 | 3 |

### DIESEL LOCOMOTIVE SUMMARY 1946 - 1988

| ORIGINAL NUMBERS | 1960 - 1988 NUMBERS | MODEL | BUILDER AND DATE | HP | QUANTITY |
|---|---|---|---|---|---|
| 1-6 | 1-6 | SW-1200 | EMD 1957 | 1200 | 6 |
| 101A, 101C | 51A, 51C | E-7A | EMD 1947 | 2000 | 2 |
| 106A, 107A, 106C, 107C | 52A, 53A, 52C, 53C | E-8A | EMD 1950 | 2250 | 4 |
| 131, 132, 133, 134, 135 | 54A, 54C, 55A, 55C, 56A | E-8A | EMD 1951 | 2250 | 5 |
| 151A, 151C - 153A, 153C | 57A, 57C - 59A, 59C | PA-1 | ALCO 1949 | 2000 | 6 |
| 154A, 154C - 157A, 157C | 60A, 60C - 63A, 63C | PA-2 | ALCO 1950-51 | 2250 | 8 |
| 121A, 121C - 124A, 124C | 78A, 78C - 81A, 81C | FP-7 | EMD 1952 | 1500 | 8 |
| 121B - 124B | 78B, 78D, 78E, 78F | F-7B | EMD 1952 | 1500 | 4 |
| 201A - 207A | 64A - 70A | F-3A | EMD 1947 | 1500 | 7 |
| 208A - 211A | 71A - 74A | F-7A | EMD 1949 | 1500 | 4 |
| 201B -207B | 64B, 64D-64H, 65B | F-3B | EMD 1947 | 1500 | 7 |
| 208B - 211B | 65D - 65G | F-7B | EMD 1949 | 1500 | 4 |
| 201C - 207C | 64C - 70C | F-3A | EMD 1947 | 1500 | 7 |
| 208C - 211C | 71C - 74C | F-7A | EMD 1949 | 1500 | 4 |
| 226A - 229A | 75A, 76A, 65H, 77A | F-7A | EMD 1949 | 1500 | 4 |
| 226B - 229B | 75B, 75D, 75E, 75F | F-9B | EMD 1955 | 1750 | 4 |
| 226C - 229C | 75C, 76C, 70C, 77C | F-7A | EMD 1949 | 1750 | 4 |
| 326A - 334A | 82A - 86A, 88A - 90A | FA-1 | ALCO 1948-49 | 1500 | 9 |
| 326C - 334C | 82C - 90C | FA-1 | ALCO 1948-49 | 1500 | 9 |
| 2ND 331AR | 87A | FA-2 | ALCO 1950 | 1600 | 1 |
| 1000 - 1010 | 22 - 32 | DS44-1000 | BALDWIN 1946-47 | 1000 | 11 |
| 1026 - 1030 | 7 - 11 | NW-2 | EMD 1947 | 1000 | 5 |
| 1201 - 1215 | 33 - 47 | S-12 | BLH 1951 | 1200 | 15 |
| 1226 - 1235 | 12 - 21 | SW-9 | EMD 1952 | 1200 | 10 |
| 1651 - 1654 | - | GE-70 TON | GE 1949-1950 | 600 | 4 |
| 1501 - 1529 | 91 - 119 | GP-7 | EMD 1950-52 | 1500 | 29 |
| 1761 - 1764 | 120 - 123 | GP-7 | EMD 1952 | 1500 | 4 |
| 1787 - 1788 | 124, 125 | AS-16 | BLH 1950 | 1600 | 2 |
| 1571 - 1586 | 126 - 141 | AS-16 | BLH 1951-53 | 1600 | 16 |
| 1701 - 1702 | 142 - 143 | RS-3 | ALCO 1951 | 1600 | 2 |
| 1551 - 1563 | 144 - 156 | RS-3 | ALCO 1950-51 | 1600 | 13 |
| 1591, 1731-1734 | 157 - 161 | H16-44 | FM 1950-51 | 1600 | 5 |
| 1655-1656 | 92 - 93 | 12 TON | WHITCOMB 1949 | 50/110 | 2 |
| 400 | 94 | 25 TON | GE 1950 | 150 | 1 |
| 20 | 20 | RDC-3 | BUDD 1956 | 275 | 1 |
| | 50 - 55 | SW-1500 | EMD 1967-68 | 1500 | 6 |
| | 56 -59 | MP-15AC | EMD 1980 | 1500 | 3 |
| | 170 - 230 | GP-40 | EMD 1966-69 | 3000 | 61 |
| | 300 - 303, 322 - 343 | GP-38 | EMD 1969-70 | 2000 | 26 |
| | 304 - 321 | GP38-2 | EMD 1973-76 | 2000 | 18 |
| | 350 - 352 | U23B | GE 1973 | 2250 | 3 |
| | 600 - 636 | SD40-2 | EMD 1978-81 | 3000 | 37 |
| | 637 | SD40-2 | MKT | 3000 | 1 |
| | 360-379 | GP39-2 | EMD 1984 | 2300 | 20 |
| | 380 - 388 | GP39-2 | EMD 1977 | 2300 | 9 |
| | 231 - 248 | GP-40 | EMD 1968 | 3000 | 18 |
| | 401B | F-38M | MKT 1975 | 2000 | 1 |
| | 500 - 501 | SLUG | MKT 1976/1982 | 1500/3000 | 2 |

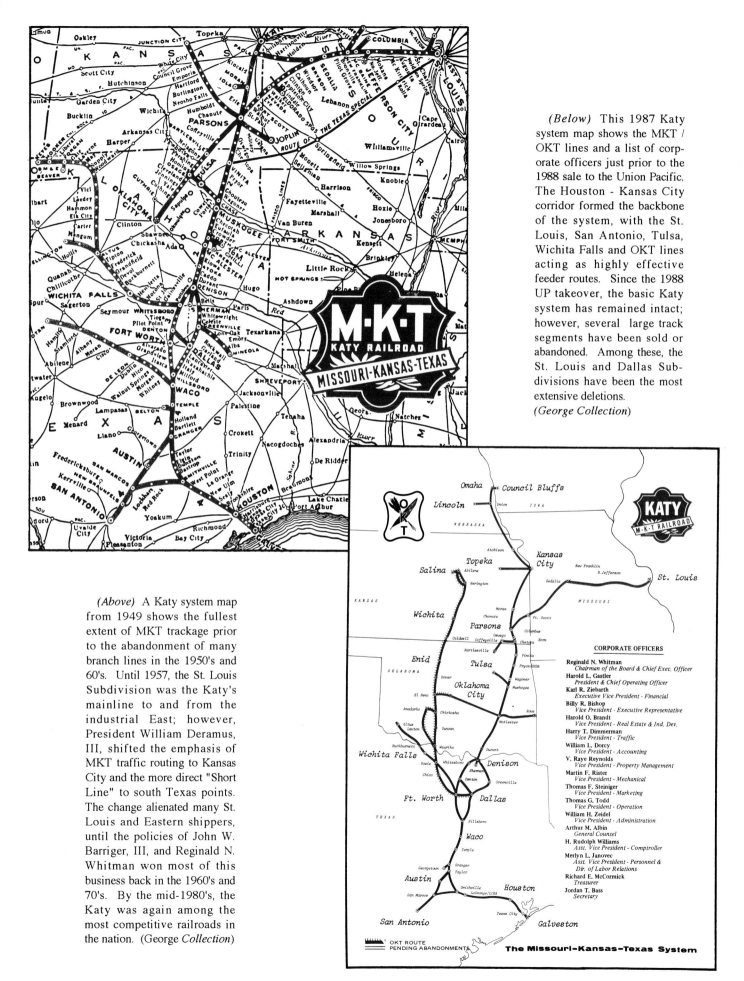

(Below) This 1987 Katy system map shows the MKT / OKT lines and a list of corporate officers just prior to the 1988 sale to the Union Pacific. The Houston - Kansas City corridor formed the backbone of the system, with the St. Louis, San Antonio, Tulsa, Wichita Falls and OKT lines acting as highly effective feeder routes. Since the 1988 UP takeover, the basic Katy system has remained intact; however, several large track segments have been sold or abandoned. Among these, the St. Louis and Dallas Subdivisions have been the most extensive deletions. (George Collection)

(Above) A Katy system map from 1949 shows the fullest extent of MKT trackage prior to the abandonment of many branch lines in the 1950's and 60's. Until 1957, the St. Louis Subdivision was the Katy's mainline to and from the industrial East; however, President William Deramus, III, shifted the emphasis of MKT traffic routing to Kansas City and the more direct "Short Line" to south Texas points. The change alienated many St. Louis and Eastern shippers, until the policies of John W. Barriger, III, and Reginald N. Whitman won most of this business back in the 1960's and 70's. By the mid-1980's, the Katy was again among the most competitive railroads in the nation. (George *Collection*)

**CORPORATE OFFICERS**

Reginald N. Whitman
*Chairman of the Board & Chief Exec. Officer*
Harold L. Gastler
*President & Chief Operating Officer*
Karl R. Ziebarth
*Executive Vice President - Financial*
Billy R. Bishop
*Vice President - Executive Representative*
Harold O. Brandt
*Vice President - Real Estate & Ind. Dev.*
Harry T. Dimmerman
*Vice President - Traffic*
William L. Dorcy
*Vice President - Accounting*
V. Raye Reynolds
*Vice President - Property Management*
Martin F. Rister
*Vice President - Mechanical*
Thomas F. Steiniger
*Vice President - Marketing*
Thomas G. Todd
*Vice President - Operation*
William H. Zeidel
*Vice President - Administration*
Arthur M. Albin
*General Counsel*
H. Rudolph Williams
*Asst. Vice President - Comptroller*
Merlyn L. Janovec
*Asst. Vice President - Personnel & Dir. of Labor Relations*
Richard E. McCormick
*Treasurer*
Jordan T. Bass
*Secretary*

**The Missouri-Kansas-Texas System**

# 1943-1945: MAIN TRAINS & MR. SLOAN

World War II brought prosperity to the Depression-weary Katy, finally enabling President Matthew Sloan to rebuild most of MKT's physical plant. Katy was called upon to carry a rapidly increasing burden of freight and passengers during the war. Heavy-goods industries which normally supplied railroad equipment were turning completely to the production of war goods, meaning Katy had to carry more and heavier loads without benefit of new equipment. Mr. Sloan attacked this problem by devising a program of repair and improvement through intensive maintenance. During the war, 6,400 freight cars and 200 passenger cars were built or repaired in the Katy's own shops.

*(Above)* Northbound No. 6, the KATY FLYER, has arrived at Greenville, Texas behind 4-6-2 Pacific Type #407 on a clear June morning in 1943. In the consist is a yellow 40 foot Katy auto car, converted to mail storage service; a Sloan-era trademark. Riding the pilot footboard, a Katy train porter handles the head end brakeman's duties. No. 407, built by Lima in 1920, wears the standard Katy locomotive paint scheme of the early 1940's, which specified a dark graphite, almost black, smoke box and stack for all engines. Without doubt, #407's most unusual feature is its wooden spoke pilot, in place of the more "Katyish" slotted steel type.

*(Opposite page, top)* A Southwestern version of Philadelphia's lush, monied suburb on the Pennsy, known as "The Main Line," was Dallas' northern suburb of Highland Park, Texas. Built in 1923, this passenger station was meticulously maintained, as was the MKT right-of-way between Highland Park and downtown Dallas; it is pictured in an early color transparency from 1942.

*(Opposite page, bottom)* The every other day mixed local, No. 54, has arrived at Greenville, Texas, from its morning run over the 50 mile Mineola Division in June 1943. Katy combination caboose #346 had been built in the company's car shops at Denison, Texas in 1942, along with nine other similar units, to accomodate passenger traffic on Katy branch lines. The local is powered by 2-6-0 Mogul #559, a 1904 product of ALCO. *(All-Arthur G. Charles, dec., John B. Charles Collection)*

Save delays -USE KATY FAST FREIGHT - It pays

*Travel and Ship Via Katy — The Southwestern Line*

13

(Opposite, above) On June 30, 1943, Katy shop forces at Parsons, Kansas completed the revision of six 1942 model Chrysler *New Yorker* automobiles that were used as inspection cars by Katy's six district superintendents. President Sloan's personal fondness for Chrysler automobiles had been expressed several years earlier in the conversion of a 1936 Chrysler *Airflow* sedan into his own M-400 inspection car, driven by a uniformed chauffeur. Similar to Mr. Sloan's glittering M-400, the *New Yorkers*, numbered M-401 to M-406, were cared for by assigned drivers stationed at each of the six district headquarters locations. Shown here, on April 27, 1944, is M-401, assigned to Superintendent C.W. Campbell of the Katy's Eastern District, headquartered at Franklin, Missouri. The cars had no steering wheels, since their flanged wheels never left the rails, and were equipped with a built-in turntable that was lowered to turn the vehicle to face the opposite direction. The cost of purchasing and revising each car was a quite reasonable $3,811.59. Five of these uniquely KATY cars were still in service as of 1956. (*L.W. Jacobs, Jr.*)

(Opposite, below) With a fresh coat of "Sloan Yellow" paint and black trim, the old Katy depot at San Marcos, Texas looked downright handsome in this view from July 1945. Located on the edge of the Texas Hill Country on the Katy's 193 mile San Antonio Division, San Marcos was fortunate to have been served by both the M-K-T and the Missouri Pacific-controlled International & Great Northern. In 1945 the town had a population of 6,000 and was the home of Southwest Texas State College, San Marcos Academy and Brown School. During World War II, nearby San Marcos Army Air Field was established as a navigational training center, resulting in quite a bit of additional activity at the Katy and IGN depots. (*Emery Gulash*)

Among the young airmen trained at San Marcos Army Air Field between May and October 1945 was Emery Gulash, a displaced Michigander, eager to expand his knowledge of Southwestern railroading and 35 mm color photography. The Katy Railroad provided ample opportunity for both, as evidenced by the following views, taken on photo safaris in the San Marcos vicinity during Emery's off-duty hours.

(Above) Under a towering plume of oil smoke, a characteristically well-groomed Pacific Type, #399, handled southbound No. 7, THE BLUEBONNET, near San Marcos in July 1945. In February that year, the Katy revised the painting standards for all its locomotives. The new scheme called for the use of a brighter metallic silver paint on the smoke box and stack, resulting in a very well-trimmed overall appearance. Riding on white-trimmed 73" drivers, #399 belonged to the graceful H-3-c Class (engines #399-408). (*Emery Gulash*)

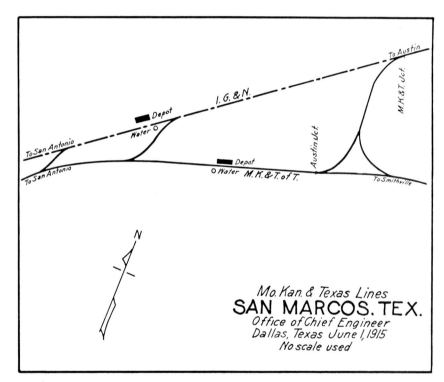

Mo. Kan. & Texas Lines
**SAN MARCOS. TEX.**
*Office of Chief Engineer
Dallas, Texas June 1, 1915
No scale used*

*(Above)* This early detour map from the Katy's Engineering Department illustrates the track layout for the MKT and IGN at San Marcos, Texas. Less than one mile northeast of the Katy depot was Austin Junction, listed as "Ajax" in World War II-era timetables. This was the junction point with the 51.5 mile San Marcos Division, which connected the Katy's San Antonio Division to the district headquarters at Smithville, Texas, on the Houston Division. In 1945, all freight trains to and from San Antonio were routed over the San Marcos Division through Smithville, with the exception of one daily fast freight that followed the Katy's more direct passenger route via Austin, Texas and 29.4 miles of joint track with the IGN. At M-K-T Junction, one half mile north of the wye at Austin Junction, or Ajax, an IGN interlocking plant protected movements to and from the joint track. *(John B. Charles Collection)*

*(Above)* Combination caboose #349 was on the southbound daylight mixed train that arrived in San Marcos from its 51.5 mile run across the San Marcos Division on this clear June afternoon in 1945. During the war and several years afterwards, two combination cabooses were assigned to the two San Marcos Division locals, indicating ridership must have been reasonably good. *(Emery Gulash)*

*(Opposite page, top)* Unmistakably KATY! Pacific #384 with No. 1, THE TEXAS SPECIAL, pauses for water under the nicely decorated water tank at San Marcos during July 1945. The green flags on the smoke box indicate this section of southbound No. 1 will be followed by yet another section. Also noticeable is #384's large 12,600 gallon capacity tender on six-wheel Commonwealth trucks. This engine belonged to Katy's H-3-a Class, built by Alco in 1916. Over 2.5 million passengers were carried on Katy trains in 1945, with gross passenger service revenue reaching $18 million. *(Emery Gulash)*

*(Opposite page, bottom)* On a beautiful September afternoon in 1945, this south-bound mixed train, No. 271, is pulling away from the San Marcos depot without pausing for water. Big-boilered Mikado #840 of the Alco-built L-2-b Class was providing ample power for this lowly fourth class train. No. 271 and its crew will work their way over the remaining 52 miles to San Antonio, handling all local chores, arriving there in the late afternoon. *(Emery Gulash)*

(Above) A veteran trainman stands next to caboose #850 in the Katy's Dallas, Texas yard on December 31, 1945. No. 850 had been constructed in the MKT's car shops, along with 29 identical way cars during 1941. Its wood body was built upon a 30'-7⅝" long steel underframe and rode on Andrews Type trucks. The company name, in script lettering, and slogan, "SERVES THE SOUTHWEST WELL," were initiated by President Sloan, as was the display of enameled metal heralds on the sides of all locomotive tenders and depots. Legend has it that Mr. Sloan overheard a brash young employee question outloud, "Where *is* that southwest well?" That remark was said to have caused the slogan to be shortened in 1946 to, "SERVES THE SOUTHWEST." The fate of the young humorist is not known. (*Arthur G. Charles*)

(*Opposite page, top*) The engineer of 2-8-2 Mikado #863 is blowing whistle signals to the towerman at the T&NO (Texas & New Orleans) interlocking at Eureka Yard on the western outskirts of Houston, Texas in November 1945. No. 863 carries the white flags of an extra and looks to be as well-maintained as any passenger engine on the Katy roster. The twenty Mikados of the L-2-c Class (engines #861-880) were built by Lima in 1920; all were originally equipped with C-1 trailer boosters that increased their tractive effort to 75025 lbs. when engaged. The heavy grades of the Houston Division between Smithville and New Ulm, Texas constantly tested Katy's medium-sized steam power, but Mike 863 appears to have been more than a match for these. (*Emery Gulash*)

(*Opposite page, bottom*) Leaving San Marcos, Texas on a July afternoon in 1945, Mikado #752 picks up speed with the daily, except Sunday, mixed local. Equipped with pilot footboards, #752 was perfectly suited to local service and belonged to the L-1-a Class (engines #701-760) built by Alco in 1913 and 1914. The rather low placement of #752's headlight on the smoke box door was uncharacteristic of engines in this class. (*Emery Gulash*)

 *The KATY — Serves the Southwest Well.*

(Above)   So pleased was Mr. Sloan with Katy's car rebuilding program that he suggested the placement of a color photograph of one of the yellow 40' mail storage cars on the back cover of the 1944 M-K-T Lines Annual Report. Fifty double-door auto cars, built by American Car & Foundry in 1937, were repainted bright yellow and equipped with air signal and steam heat lines for use as headend cars in high speed passenger service during the war. In 1945, the Katy shops constructed an additional 39 mail storage cars, which matched the earlier group. (*author's collection*)

19

(Above) The northbound fourth class mixed train, No. 270, began its day at San Antonio's Sloan Yard at 8:00 AM; it is shown here in the early afternoon, entering the 24 car siding at San Marcos, Texas to wait for its southbound counterpart, No. 271. As usual, the south Texas sky on that September day was filled with billowy cumulus clouds, produced by weather conditions in the nearby Gulf of Mexico. During that first week of September, 1945, the war in the Pacific finally came to an end on the 2nd, known as "VJ Day" because of the formal surrender of the last major Axis power, Japan, to Allied forces.

(Below) Same date. What now, brown cow? A gate at the stock pens in the distance to the right was apparently left unhooked by cattle shippers, resulting in this interesting scene. Brown Bossy watches while northbound No. 270 is in the hole and as southbound No. 271 eases down the mainline to the San Marcos depot behind Mikado #840. The foreground at left offers a close-up look at northbound #848's 61" drivers and Walschaert valve gear. No. 848 had a tractive effort of 63900 lbs., otherwise designated by the Katy as a 64% engine. Mikado #840, with this same train No. 271, was also pictured on page 17. (Both- Emery Gulash)

*(Above)*   Known as a "Grab Shot" by photographers, some subject matter is simply too good to resist shooting, no matter how unconventional the camera angle or focus might be. Such a photo opportunity presented itself to photographer Gulash as a formation of Beech AT-7 navigational trainers passed overhead at San Marcos en route to San Antonio to join a mass fly-over to celebrate the end of World War II. The AT-7s were stationed at nearby San Marcos Army Air Field, which was served by the Katy on its San Marcos Division.   As soon as the flight had passed, thoughts returned quickly to shooting Mikado #848 and the mixed local.

*(Below)*   The crew of northbound mixed local No. 270 appears to have broken for lunch at a nearby beanery on that same September day.   Before departing to shoot Missouri Pacific action across town on the IGN line, photographer Gulash concentrated on filling the frame of his Zeiss-Ikon Contax III 35 mm camera with the engine, five cars and caboose of the mixed local.   Kodachrome 10 was used for all of Emery's 1945-era slides and he was indeed fortunate the Contax III had a newly introduced built-in light meter, which made it one of the most advanced cameras of its day. *(Both- Emery Gulash)*

(Top) Laboring under an oily black cloud of its own making, this train appears to be the northbound way freight at San Marcos, Texas in May 1945. In addition to the activity of four daily passenger trains in each direction, extras, way freights and mixed locals, a daily hot freight, Nos. 80 and 81, officially named THE KATY KOMET, blew through San Marcos in the peaceful pre-dawn at 5:15 each day; northbound No. 80 roared by each night at 8:30. THE KOMET had the distinction of being the only Katy freight train to use the 29 mile section of IGN joint track between San Marcos and Austin, Texas, that Katy passsenger trains had used since 1905. All other freight tonnage was moved over the San Marcos Division through Smithville, which was 35 miles longer than the route via Austin. M-K-T management calculated the savings in joint track expenses was worth the increased train mileage and operating time. This policy began to change after 1957, when tumbling revenues and declining track conditions caused new management to view the expanded use of trackage rights as the only alternative to costly maintenance-of-way expenses on the San Antonio and San Marcos Divisions. (Emery Gulash)

(Opposite page, top) The same #716, as seen above, was in action in September 1945 with this southbound extra, crossing York Creek, seven miles south of San Marcos, Texas. The forty-three 2-8-2s of the L-1-a Class were the backbone of the Katy's power roster, having superheated extended wagon top boilers with a working pressure of 195 lbs. The overall length of the engine and tender was 78'-6", with a total weight of 455,500 lbs. (Emery Gulash)

(Opposite page, bottom) During 1944, 336 buildings were painted and repaired by the Katy; among these was the classic tile-roofed structure at Kincaid, Kansas, exactly 82 miles south of Kansas City. The "Sloan Yellow" station is neatly trimmed with dark green, rather than the more common black used during that period. This photo was snapped September 1, 1956 and demonstrates that Katy's high maintenance standards were still in evidence at that date. (H.D. Killam)

(Above) "Sloan Yellow" water tank car #X-16727 was among 55 such cars employed by the Katy in 1945 for company service; it is seen here at Houston, Texas, in November of that year, bracketed by work train bunk cars. A hand pump was placed on top of the tank for the convenience of the laborers, who probably emptied this tank with great regularity in the blazing summertime heat of south Texas. The overall length of this car was 34', riding on arch bar trucks with Cardwell draft gear. (Emery Gulash)

(Above) On its route to Kansas City, Missouri, northbound No. 4, THE KATY LIMITED, has made its scheduled stop at San Marcos, Texas at 1:22 on a perfect July afternoon in 1945. THE LIMITED paused at any station in Texas to pick up or discharge passengers and handled only four passenger cars (sleeper, parlor car, diner and chair car) between San Antonio and the crew change point at Waco, Texas. Heavyweight headend equipment comprised over half THE LIMITED's consist, including a yellow mail storage box car and a refrigerated express car of Rio Grande Valley produce, on this warm summer's day. The real star of the show was big 4-6-2 #395 of the H-3-b Class (engines #389-398), built by Alco in 1917; its spotless appearance was the embodiment of KATY pride and high maintenance standards.

Katy L-1-a Class Mikado freight locomotives were the workhorses of the railroad and could also be used in passenger service when necessary. This advertising art, dating from 1928, depicts a Katy "Mike" in such use.

(Opposite, above) Crossing the San Marcos River, northeast of the town of San Marcos, southbound No. 7, THE BLUEBONNET, has reached the north switch of the twenty-four car passing siding at milepost 985.9. No. 7 has just come off the IGN joint track, which was equipped with automatic block signals. For the next forty-one miles THE BLUEBONNET was operated entirely by timetable, train orders and the MKT's book of rules, until reaching the outskirts of San Antonio where block signals were again used. On that beautiful, but warm, July 1945 afternoon, No. 7 was powered by high-stepping Pacific Type #398 that had a working pressure of 210 lbs. and a tractive effort of 42750 lbs.

(Opposite, below) On a bright June day in 1945, the southbound daylight mixed train has arrived at San Marcos on its run from the division point terminal at Smithville, Texas. Beautifully maintained Mikado #734 had been built by Alco in 1913 and was originally a coal burner. By March 1, 1945, all of MKT's 312 locomotives were oil burners, the result of a tremendous surge in oil production in the Katy-served Southwest during World War II.
(All- Emery Gulash)

24

**Katy Builds**
**FOR A GREATER SOUTHWEST**

# The Building Bill — $100,000,000

A *new* and *finer* Katy now serves the Southwest!

Within the past four years nearly a hundred million dollars have been put back into Katy properties to afford the most efficient rail transportation the Southwest has ever enjoyed.

In spite of serious shortages of men and materials, every inch of main-line road bed has been reballasted.... Nearly 350 miles of new steel have been laid ... 4,500,000 creosoted cross ties installed ... 900 locomotives given heavy repairs or rebuilt ... Revenue freight cars in bad order reduced

to 3/10 of 1 percent of ownership—a record "low" in the Company's history.... All passenger equipment has been repaired and renovated....Stations, service buildings and bridges strengthened, repaired and painted, and many other improvement projects completed. And the Katy's record of good housekeeping is outstanding.

All this without a borrowed penny—and at the same time the mortgage debt was being reduced approximately $40,000,000.

The Katy *is* building to keep pace with the new and greater Southwest.

**M·K·T**
**Katy Lines**

**MISSOURI-KANSAS-TEXAS** **RAILROAD COMPANY**

**M·K·T**
**DIAMOND**
**ANNIVERSARY**
**1870 ◇ 1945**

*(Left)* This advertisement was published and circulated in June 1945, in connection with the Katy Railroad's 75th, "Diamond Anniversary," celebration. Due to illness, President Matthew Sloan was unable to deliver a speech at Denison, Texas on June 11, 1945; instead, it was read aloud to the crowd at the official celebration and listed, with great pride, the many accomplishments of the eleven year Sloan presidency. Only three days afterwards, Mr. Sloan died of a cerebral hemorrhage in a New York hospital, where he was undergoing treatment. The war in Europe with Nazi Germany had ended on May 8, 1945, while the conflict with Japan raged on. After the destruction of Hiroshima and Nagasaki with atomic bombs during August 1945 and the surrender of Japan on September 2, 1945, an unparalleled era of prosperity began for the U.S. economy and the Katy. *(author's collection)*

# 1946-1953: KATY'S FINEST HOUR

Chairman Raymond Morfa and President Donald Fraser carried Matthew Sloan's work forward after his sudden death in 1945, with systemwide dieselization at the top of the post-war priority list. In August 1946 the first two diesel units arrived; these being Baldwin Model DS44-1000 switchers, appropriately numbered 1000 and 1001, assigned to the Dallas, Texas yard. Katy's two colorful and highly publicized EMD E-7A passenger units, numbered 101A and 101C, arrived in March of 1947 to join look-alike Frisco units in powering the joint TEXAS SPECIAL. MKT's first diesel freight power was acquired in 1947, consisting of seven EMD F-3 A-B-A sets. As the diesels entered service, the systematic retirement of all steam power began. This "Twilight" period of Katy steam and diesel power was an interesting mixture of the old and new that was fortunately recorded by a few dedicated photographers. Maintenance standards and employee morale were extremely high throughout this memorable era.

*(Above)* Riding the 90 foot turntable at the Franklin, Missouri roundhouse on September 15, 1946, is 2-8-2 Mikado Type #735 of the L-1-a Class. During World War II, L-1-a Mikados handled 100-car oil tank trains between Franklin and St. Louis on the almost gradeless 189 mile St. Louis Division, built along the northern bank of the Missouri River. On the line between Franklin and Sedalia, Missouri, tonnage ratings dropped nearly 50%, due to the hilly terrain south of the Missouri River, necessitating the use of Mikados in assigned helper service on this section. *(L.W. Jacobs, Jr.)*

*(Opposite page, top)* KATY'S BEST ON PARADE! The twelve "Pullman Green" cars of No. 2, THE TEXAS SPECIAL, are being wheeled northward near San Marcos, Texas in elegant fashion by gleaming Pacific Type #405 on this September morning in 1945. On July 7, 1946, through sleeping car service on THE TEXAS SPECIAL was inaugurated from San Antonio to New York and Washington D.C., in connection with the New York Central, the Pennsylvania and the Baltimore & Ohio railroads. *(Emery Gulash)*

(Above) In July 1948, USRA 0-8-0 switcher #59 plies the rails of the Houston, Texas industrial district. Katy assigned three big 0-8-0s to Houston that summer, along with one of the new 1000 HP diesels. No. 59 was built by Alco in 1923, had a tractive effort of 53,950 lbs. and rode on 51" drivers. Engines #59-68, of the C-1-b Class, were distingushed from earlier Katy 0-8-0s by their jaunty smokebox-mounted bells and Walschaert valve gear. Was any steam switcher in the Southwest ever as obviously well-maintained in daily service as Katy's #59? (Frank Watson)

(Opposite page, top) This painting was commissioned by the state of Oklahoma for the cover of its 1989 state railroad map, commemorating the famous Land Run of 1889. A north-bound local is pictured near Stringtown, Oklahoma, passing milepost 600, circa 1947. With the exception of the Kansas City Division, all milepost markers on the M-K-T's mainline displayed the precise distance from Union Station at St. Louis, Missouri. Motive power for the little local was provided by a Katy classic: Mikado #706, of the L-1-a Class. (Painting by Raymond B. George, Jr.)

(Opposite page, bottom) Mikado #743 was found by the water tank at Fayette, Missouri, while detouring on Katy's 35 mile Moberly Subdivision in 1948. The 66-pound rail of this branch was sorely tested by heavy mainline Mikados when occasional Missouri River flooding interrupted service on the St. Louis Division. Detouring trains made connections with the Wabash Railroad at Moberly, Missouri for an alternate dry route into St. Louis. ( L.W. Jacobs, Jr.)

(Above) In 1935, when "Steam Was King" on the Katy Lines, this public timetable was issued that pictured an art deco-style rendition of 4-6-2 Pacific Type #400. (George Collection)

*(Above)* Late in 1945, the Katy and Frisco placed an order with EMD for two E-7 A-A sets to power their new joint streamlined glamour train, THE TEXAS SPECIAL, but it would not be until March 1947 that the Katy's two diesel units, #101A and #101C, arrived. The E-7s were then exhibited across the Katy system and briefly tested by the mechanical department before regular service began. Katy's units were quite similar to Frisco's, except for the placement of the M-K-T herald ahead of the Frisco emblem on the forward side panels, as pictured here in May 1947 at Greenville, Texas with No. 2, the northbound TEXAS SPECIAL. Frisco reversed the arrangement of emblems on their E-7 units.

*(Below)* Same date, Greenville, Texas. As in the steam era, a rotating pool was carefully maintained that balanced the mileage of Katy and Frisco power and crews. Normally, the Katy's E-7s operated between Muskogee, Oklahoma and San Antonio, Texas, with Frisco power used between St. Louis and Muskogee. However, in order to balance mileage, Katy units were occasionally operated into St. Louis, and, likewise, Frisco units made visits as far south as San Antonio.
*(Both photos -Arthur G. Charles)*

# The Texas Special

(Above)  A cherished souvenir from a glorious day for the Katy Railroad is this first day cover issued and stamped aboard northbound No. 2, the streamlined TEXAS SPECIAL, on May 15, 1948, the first day of regular service between St. Louis and San Antonio. This was only one of many promotions used to publicize and promote the glittering new "Flagship of the Southwest" for Katy and Frisco. The dieselized SPECIAL originally handled 11 cars from the Frisco connection at Vinita, Oklahoma, to Denison, Texas, then split off a 3-car Ft. Worth section and added a diner. Three sleepers were dropped at Dallas, leaving seven cars for the final leg of the trip to San Antonio. Turnaround time for this same power and equipment at San Antonio was a brief two hours, before departure with northbound No. 2. (George Collection)

For a year after delivery in 1947, the new E-7s handled standard heavyweight consists, due to a delay in the construction of the matching passenger equipment. Two 14-car sets of streamlined cars, built by Pullman Standard, arrived in April 1948 but the first official revenue run of the shiny new all-streamlined TEXAS SPECIAL was on May 15, 1948. Katy and Frisco had been operating THE TEXAS SPECIAL jointly since March of 1917, but this famous train had originated as an all-Katy affair in 1915, traveling its entire route from St. Louis to San Antonio on Katy rails. The more direct joint arrangement prevailed until January 4, 1959, when the contract with the Frisco for the operation of THE TEXAS SPECIAL was discontinued and service to St. Louis ended. The Katy then shifted THE TEXAS SPECIAL to a Kansas City-San Antonio routing, thus abolishing THE BLUEBONNET, and eventually shorted this to a Kansas City-Dallas run in 1964, before all Katy passenger service ended on June 30, 1965.

(Below)  General Motors Electro Motive Division builder's painting of Katy E-7 A-A units #101A and #101C. Apart from the distinctive star and lettering on their noses, these units were the only Katy diesels to wear stainless steel fluting on their sides. The contrast between art and reality becomes apparent when this painting and the photography on the opposite page are compared. The Katy's E-7s were originally painted a brilliant red orange, quite unlike the red of the builder's painting. Due to the heavy use of these units in the first years of their service, it became impossible to maintain the original paint scheme. By 1951, the TEXAS SPECIAL lettering and small Frisco emblems had disappeared and the trucks were painted a more conservative black. (George Collection)

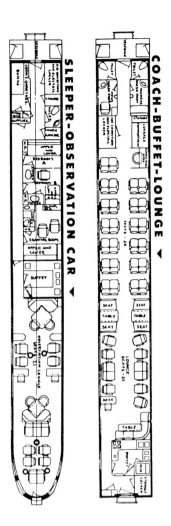

SLEEPER-OBSERVATION CAR ▼

COACH-BUFFET-LOUNGE ▼

THE NEWEST comfort innovation for Katy's Texas Special patrons is this gay and charming lounge, a beautifully furnished car with new, unusual, delightful features.

Cushioned divans, tables for refreshments, plenty of room for reading and smoking. A writing desk where you can drop a line to your loved ones. And ever-present, a courteous Texas Special attendant.

The *Streamlined* Texas Special...Observation-Lounge Car

*(Above)* Katy public timetables were among the most handsomely designed and printed during the post war era. Little expense was spared to produce this thirty page table, in effect as of December 1, 1948. Shown on the back cover was an interior view of sleeper-observation car #1400, the *Steven F. Austin*, named for the "Father of the Republic of Texas." When President Harry Truman required transportation between his Independence, Missouri home and Texas points, he always traveled via the M-K-T, aboard #1400, reserved for his exclusive use. The Frisco counterpart of #1400 was #1350, the *Joseph Pulitzer*. These beautiful cars were available only to first class Pullman patrons, with service provided by Pullman porters and waiters.

*(Below, right)* The front cover of the same 1948 timetable pictured the interior of coach-buffet-lounge #1300, named for a president of the Republic of Texas, *Mirabeau B. Lamar*. No. 1300 was accessible to all passengers aboard THE TEXAS SPECIAL, with service provided by Katy waiters. Frisco's version of the same car was #1650, the *Sterling Price*. Soft drinks, tobacco products, confections, sandwiches, etc. were served on the lounge cars; however, Texas statutes restricted the sale of alcoholic beverages to Missouri and Oklahoma.
*(Both-Michael Warden Thomas Collection)*

KATY KATY

M·K·T KATY RAILROAD
MISSOURI-KANSAS-TEXAS

M·K·T KATY RAILROAD
MISSOURI-KANSAS-TEXAS

TIME TABLES TIME TABLES

CORRECTED TO DECEMBER 1, 1948          CORRECTED TO DECEMBER 1, 1948
FORM 1-125    PRINTED IN U. S. A.       FORM 1-125    PRINTED IN U. S. A.

*(Right, above)* An assortment of colorful Katy public timetables dating from 1946 to 1953 demonstrates the heavy emphasis placed on publicizing the new streamlined TEXAS SPECIAL, especially the EMD E-7 A-A diesels. The new equipment and advertising methods were very effective, with passenger service revenues on the Katy Lines holding at a very steady $4.5 million annually during the non-war years 1947 - 1950. *(author's collection)*

*(Right, below)* In 1948 this postcard was distributed by the Katy's Passenger Traffic Department to potential customers of the TEXAS SPECIAL. *(author's collection)*

*(Below)* The startling brightness of the TEXAS SPECIAL paint scheme lightens up this normally drab view from the 11th Street overpass at St. Louis Union Station on September 5, 1953. In the foreground is RPO baggage car #1000, named for the last president of the Republic of Texas, *Anson B Jones*; this was MKT's only streamlined headend car. Behind #1000 is a Frisco RPO, either the *Rock Hill* or *Normandy*. Due to the limited number of streamlined RPO baggage cars, standard heavyweight headend cars were used from the outset to supplement streamlined equipment. *(Al Chione Collection)*

(Above)   No. 1651 has arrived with the mixed local, No. 54, at Greenville, Texas in June, 1949, having completed its 50 mile run from Mineola, Texas. Katy acquired a sampling of diesel power from a sizeable number of early builders, including four 600 horsepower 70-ton units from General Electric, numbered 1651 through 1654. MKT earmarked these diminutive switchers for limited yard work and mixed service on light density branch lines. No. 1651 was successfully tested during 1949 on the Mineola local, where its performance prompted the Katy to order a slight increase in the tractive effort of the three latter units. As were all early Katy diesel switchers, #1651 was painted gray with black and white horizontal stripes. Nos. 1652 - 1654 arrived in 1950;

however, these, and subsequent new diesels, were painted red with yellow warning stripes.

(Below)   Katy 2-8-2 Mikado Type #902 pauses for a moment as a Kansas City Southern freight train powered by a colorful F-7 lash-up rolls through the joint MKT/KCS Hunt Yard at Greenville, Texas, in January 1950. By 1950, 119 diesel locomotives had been acquired by the Katy, while 175 steam engines remained in service at the end of that year. Heavy mainline power such as #902, built by Lima in 1923, was being equipped with pilot footboards in order to be more versatile during the last days of Katy steam.
*(Both-Arthur G. Charles)*

(Above) Wisps of lovely stratus clouds float above this scene at Hunt Yard, Greenville, Texas, as 2-6-0 Mogul Type #483 prepares for its 6:30 AM departure with train No. 53, the southbound Mineola Local, on a cool February morning in 1951. The field in the foreground is plowed and ready for cotton or peanut planting in the spring. The rich soil surrounding this train's destination, Mineola, Texas, was famous for its annual peach, watermelon and spinach harvests. No. 483, of Katy's J-5 Class, had been built in 1902 by Alco; however, in 1907 it was completely rebuilt with another boiler in the Katy shops for unknown reasons. The J-5 Moguls had a very nicely balanced appearance, with large wagon-top boilers and distinctive smokebox-mounted bells. (Arthur G. Charles)

(Below) With its cab curtain buttoned, Katy 0-6-0 yard goat #13 handles the chores on the caboose track at Franklin, Missouri, on a brisk yet beautiful morning in 1950. Built by Baldwin in 1911 and of Katy's B-1 Class, these switchers had a tractive effort of 28,700 pounds, making for the uniquely Katy designation of a 29% engine. One of the oldest settlements west of the Mississippi, Franklin was an operating hub for the Katy Railroad and home for many crews working on the Sedalia and St. Louis Divisions and branch lines to Moberly and Columbia, Missouri. (D. Ellis Chester, dec., Helen Chester Collection)

(Above) When not used to clean up derailments, wrecker #X-101220 was kept in steam at the Katy's Parsons, Kansas reclamation plant for heavy duty lifting chores, as seen here in 1952. The Katy had eleven separate wrecker outfit trains stationed at various division points systemwide. No. X-101220 was assigned to Parsons, as were the following wrecker outfit cars: 1 ex-troop sleeper, 1 kitchen diner, 1 convoy car, 1 block & tool car, 2 rail & tie cars, 2 tool cars and 1 tank car for water. Each of Katy's six districts employed a small army of track workers, for normal right-of-way maintenance, that were called upon in emergency situations to man the wrecker outfit train and get the mainline back into service. No. X-101220 was a coal burning 120 ton self-propelled crane, built in 1916 by Industrial Works of Bay City, Michigan. (C.A. Snarrenberg)

(Top) 0-8-0 switch engine #43 was found in the Katy's City Yard at Houston, Texas, in December 1947. In 1920, the M.K.&T. acquired twenty 0-8-0s, numbered 39-58, from the Lima Locomotive Works, of Lima, Ohio. These were the earliest and most numerous of Katy's heavy duty steam switchers, having Baker valve gear and Ragonnet power reverse, classified as C-1-a 54% engines. The original working boiler pressure of 175 lbs. was later raised to 185 lbs., making for a tractive effort of 53,950 lbs. By 1947 all units of this class were oil burners, with the exception of coal burner #50. stationed at Ray Yard, Denison, Texas. (Frank Watson)

(Opposite page, top) 2-8-2 Mikado Type #723 kicks the dust from the crossovers with a northbound local at Houston in July 1948. At that time fifteen 57% "Mikes" were assigned to through and local service on the South Texas District, headquartered at Smithville, Texas. The head end crew of the local appear intent upon catching any passing breeze from atop #723's tender as their only means to cool off in the sweltering Gulf Coast heat. This beautifully maintained Mikado was of Katy's L-1-a Class (engines #701-740), built by Alco in 1913. These easy firing oil-burners had extended wagon top boilers with a working pressure of 195 lbs. All had Walschaert valve gear and 61" drivers, with a tractive effort of 57,250 lbs. (Robert T. Fillman)

(Opposite page, bottom) Little 0-6-0 #36 was a veteran of 37 years on the M-K-T, when photographed at Houston, Texas in December 1947. At that time this switcher was leased to the Port Terminal Railroad Association, which accounts for its somewhat less that normal "Katyish" spit and polish appearance. Ten engines, numbered 29-38, were included in the Katy's B-2 Class, built by American Locomotive Co.'s Manchester Works in 1910. No. 36 was retired in August 1951 and sold, along with 17 other steam engines, to Luria Brothers & Co. of Granite City, Illinois, to be scrapped, in March 1952. (Robert T. Fillman)

THE Katy LIMITED
20½ HOURS
from SAN ANTONIO

36

*(Above)* At Greenville, Texas on July 8, 1953, the last Katy steam engine in service, J-5 Class Mogul #508, appears ready for use on the Mineola local; however, its replacement, GE switcher #1652, at the extreme left, was already handling that job. No. 508 (Alco, 1903) would remain in service as backup power during 1953, but was eventually scrapped in 1954. The most noticeable item on #508 was the bright M-K-T emblem on its tender; it is that item, above all others, that observers of the Katy seem to recall most vividly about this road's steam era power. *(Arthur G. Charles)*

*(Opposite, top)* A brand new EMD GP-7 road switcher, #1509, was found in tow at Franklin, Missouri, on March 20, 1950. The new engine was taken to Parsons, Kansas, where it was fully checked out prior to entering revenue service. Before purchasing new diesel units, it was Katy's practice to thoroughly evaluate demonstrators on several districts to determine tonnage ratings and operating capabilities. Such tests were a common occurrence at Franklin Yard, due to the hills on the line between Franklin and Sedalia, Missouri, which were the ruling north and southbound grades on the system. No. 1509 was later renumbered 99 in 1960 and completed 38 years of service with the Katy, before being sold by the Union Pacific in 1989. *(D. Ellis Chester)*

*(Opposite, bottom)* Three Katy steam engines await their fate at the Dallas, Texas downtown yard on January 21, 1952. Pacific Type #408, Mogul #587 and 0-6-0 switcher #25 were three of 113 steam locomotives owned by the Katy at the beginning of 1952. By the end of that year, only 39 steamers would still survive. Visible in the distance to the right, are a new GP-7 and an Alco FA unit, being readied for their next assignments. *(Arthur G. Charles)*

*(Below)* Probably the most unusual locomotive ever used on the Katy Railroad was #4000, nicknamed "The Blue Goose," a huge oil-burning single unit gas turbine built by Westinghouse/Baldwin. The main generator powered four AAR Type B 4-wheel trucks, resulting in a 4,000 HP unit equal in power to a pair of Alco PA-1s. No. 4000 is pictured at Franklin, Missouri, date unknown. During tests in 1952, this beast made numerous appearances across the system in regular passenger service. The most well-remembered test was a series of trips between Denison, Texas and Parsons, Kansas with northbound No. 6, THE KATY FLYER, and the southbound return runs to Denison with No. 7, the crack BLUEBONNET. The operating routines of these trains were quite different, with No. 6 making frequent stops for passengers, mail and express, while No. 7 was an expedited train with few in-between stops. The runs on the Oklahoma corridor afforded a wide variety of operating situations for testing #4000; however, the Katy appears to have been more concerned with maintenance problems, rather than performance statistics, and opted not to purchase the unit. *(D.Ellis Chester)*

*(Above)* North and south bound freight trains were built, taken apart, classified and switched at Ray Yard, on the western outskirts of Denison, Texas, the geographical center of the Katy Railroad. In the late winter of 1954, EMD FP-7 #122C, built in January 1952, appears ready for its next freight haul at the open air two stall servicing shelter, adjacent to the Ray Yard roundhouse. Although #122C was usually in freight service, Katy's eight FP-7 units and four F-7 B units were equipped with steam generating boilers for dual service, passenger or freight, use. The tractive effort of a 3-unit 4500 HP FP-7–F-7B–FP-7 lash-up was a hefty 187,500 pounds.

*(Below)* Same date. Denison's 22-stall roundhouse was second in size only to the large Parsons, Kansas enginehouse, having been constructed in 1923 in connection with the rebuilding of Ray into a massive double hump classification yard. By 1954, most Katy yards had become obsolete and needed to be modernized; however, 100% diseleization had been attained, with a total of 212 road and switching units in service that year. Several of the bright new diesels were in the roundhouse this day, including EMD GP-7 #1525 and two Alco freight A-units. *(Both photos- Carl A. Snarrenberg)*

*(Above)* At the Denison, Texas Ray Yard roundhouse in 1954, BLH Model S-12 switcher #1214 is in perfect mid-morning lighting to display the company's safety slogan, neatly lettered on the long hoods of all standard yard power. The slogan was part of a concerted effort by management and labor that led to the presentation of the E. H. Harriman Gold Medal Award to the Katy on September 17, 1953 for its 1952 safety record; the best among all Class A railroads. Fourteen S-12 units were delivered in 1951, with #1214 remaining unmodified until its trade in to EMD in 1968. As with most early Katy diesels, these 1200 HP units were originally numbered in relationship to their horsepower rating, i.e., 1201-1215.

*(Below)* Same date. EMD SW-9 #1229 works the tracks near the Katy car shops in downtown Denison, Texas. Ten 1200 HP SW-9s came to the MKT in 1952, numbered 1226-1235, and were renumbered 12-21 in 1960. All remained in service until final disposition in 1986-87, with the exception of unlucky #13 which was wrecked and disposed of in 1967. The pictured engine and several other Katy SW-9s are still in service as this is written in 1993 on south Texas shortlines Georgetown Railroad (#16 & #17) and Austin Northwestern Railroad (#14 & #15).
*(Both photos- Carl A. Snarrenberg)*

41

*(Above)* RS-3 #1560 was found in yard service at Parsons, Kansas, on May 28, 1955. Katy received six 1600 HP Alco RS-3s in 1950, and another nine units in 1951, numbered 1551-1563 and 1701-1702. The two latter units were equipped with steam boilers for use as auxiliary branch line passenger power. These fifteen RS-3s were used for local and mixed service, also in the larger yards for heavy duty switching chores. Their powerful General Electric Type-4 traction motors and GT 581 main generator were able to quickly develop a tractive effort in excess of 60,000 pounds, making them very popular with yard crews. *(Howard Killam)*

*(Top)* In matters of art, the Katy had its very own "Old Master," namely Mr. Howard Fogg of Boulder, Colorado. In 1951, Katy management was so pleased with the Alco builder's painting of RS-3 #1551 by a young Howard Fogg, that additional copies were acquired and placed in each district office on the system. Artist Fogg's first encounter with the Katy had been on a railfan weekend trip in April 1950 to Parsons, Kansas. It was here at Parsons, while talking with veteran enginemen and observing Katy's well-maintained motive power and facilities first-hand, that Mr. Fogg acquired his life long affection for the M-K-T. He sums up his admiration simply by saying, "The Katy had Class!"

Howard Fogg's masterly craftsmanship is evident in the watercolor painting above and in a now famous series done ten years later for his friend and benefactor, Katy president John W. Barriger, III. *(Alco print, George Collection, with permission of Howard Fogg)*

(Above)  Steam generator-equipped Baldwin AS-16 road switcher #1787 at Franklin, Missouri, on July 4, 1953. The Katy had a fondness for Baldwin switching power early on, with eleven Model DS44-1000 units arriving in 1946-47 and an additional fifteen 1200 horsepower Model S-12 "goats" built in 1951. Katy sampled Baldwin's new 1600 horsepower general purpose Model AS-16s in 1950 with an order for 8 units, numbered 1571-1578. Six more AS-16s were delivered in 1951, numbered 1579-1584. The last group of AS-16s arrived from Baldwin early in 1953, consisting of two standard engines, numbered 1585 and 1586, along with two dual service units equipped with boilers, numbered 1787 and 1788. The total order of AS-16 road switchers amounted to 18 units, becoming the last power acquired from Baldwin-Lima-Hamilton by the Katy. *(Arthur G. Charles)*

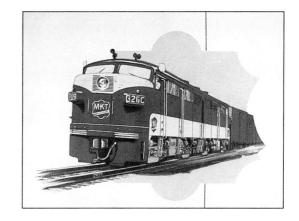

(Below)  A crewman inserts white extra flags on the nose of AS-16 #1579 at Lindale, Missouri in 1953, as the engine is fueled, sanded and watered in preperation to depart for a day of local work and switching on nearby coal mining spurs. Lindale was a fuel and water stop on the Katy's Sedalia Division, also a breakfast stop for southbound No. 5, THE KATY FLYER. *(C.A.Snarrenberg)*

(Above)  In addition to painting Katy's Alco RS-3 series, artist Howard Fogg earlier painted the portrait of Katy's Alco FA-1s for the builder in 1949. In 1955, a two-color adaptation of Mr. Fogg's original painting was used for the cover of the M-K-T Annual Report, shown here. *(George Collection)*

The Katy acquired eighteen 1500 HP FA-1 road units from Alco in 1948-49, numbered 326A-334A and 326C-334C. These nine double A lash-ups were rarely separated from their mates during the first years of their operation. Tragically, on October 21, 1950, a firey crossing accident with freight train No. 281 and a gasoline tank truck, at San Marcos, Texas, killed three Katy crewmen and totally destroyed FA-1 #331A. Its mate, #331C was towed to the Katy shops at Bellmead, Texas and underwent extensive repairs before returning to service in the spring of 1952, paired with new FA-2 #331AR, the only FA-2 owned by the MKT. The letter "R" denoted "replacement" on Katy roster books.

(Above)   Passengers from No. 6, the northbound KATY FLYER, wait on the station platform of the massive Parsons, Kansas passenger station on a warm and windy evening in the summer of 1953.   The northbound FLYER was split into Kansas City  and St. Louis sections at Parsons, with  arrivals set for  9:25 PM, that same evening at K.C., and 7:30 AM next morning in St. Louis.  If these schedules were not met, a letter of explanation had to be on President Donald Fraser's desk in St. Louis the following morning.  On the first floor of the Parsons station, with its windows shaded by awnings, was the always-open Union News cafe, where FLYER passengers could enjoy a good hot meal before climbing back on board their respective trains for the remainder of the trip northward.

This impressive station and district office building dominated the business district of downtown Parsons, having been completed and opened for service on January 9, 1914; sadly, it was demolished by the Katy in the mid-1960's, after divisional headquarters had been consolidated at Denison, Texas. (C. A. Snarrenberg)

(Below)  Fourteen miles south of Parsons was the 24-hour telegraph station at Oswego, Kansas, on the Katy's Cherokee Division, as it was on June 18, 1955.  As with the Parsons station, its clean-cut lines were characteristic of stations designed and built by the Katy between 1912 and 1926, during the presidency of Charles E. Schaff. (Howard Killam)

(Above)  This view of the Parsons Locomotive Shops, taken July 9, 1973, shows only a small portion of the Katy's investment at this point.  This facility alone employed from 300 to 500 men in the late 1940's, when it was converted to diesel maintenance and extensively modernized.  As early as 1870, when Parsons was founded by the M.K.&T. Railway, the main locomotive shops of the Katy were located here.  A second major engine facility at Bellmead, Texas was downgraded when the Parsons shops were chosen to be the Katy's primary diesel servicing center in 1949.
(Earl Holloway)

(Below)  Several sets of Alco PAs were in the Parsons Locomotive Shops this day in 1952, still wearing their as-purchased paint scheme.  Noticeable atop the cab of this unknown PA is a dazzling array of five blended forward air horns and one rear horn.  The Katy equipped approximately one-third of its Alco and EMD passenger power with similar horn arrangements.  The Parsons Mechanical Department was well known for its fascination with developing unique engine signaling devices, as in the steam era when Katy passenger and freight power were said to have the most pleasing and distinctive whistle tones in the Southwest. (C.A. Snarrenberg)

*(Above)* GP-7 #1505, at Paola, Kansas on September 1, 1956. This engine was assigned to the mixed local, Nos. 55 and 54, that operated on the Katy's 86 mile Holden Subdivision between Bryson, Missouri and Paola, Kansas. Known as "The High Line," the Holden Subdivision linked the Sedalia and St. Louis Divisions with the Kansas City Division and had been used originally as a short route between St. Louis and Kansas City. Visible behind #1505 at Paola, is the turntable used to turn the power of the mixed local for its return trip. Unfortunately, this line's days were numbered by this date, due to a decline in traffic and an increase in maintenance expenses, which resulted in its abandonment in 1958. *(Howard Killam)*

*(Right)* At Denison, Texas, in 1951, EMD F-7 #227A receives attention at an improvised diesel sanding station. This F-7 was equipped with two-way radio, as evidenced by the large Bendix "wagon-wheel" antenna on the cab roof. The Katy pioneered the use of radio communications in yard engines in 1947 and had installed end-to-end radio on diesel-powered mainline freight trains by April 1948. By 1951, the primitive Bendix antennas were being replaced by less conspicious devices. *(C. A. Snarrenberg)*

*(Opposite, above)* With its Bendix radio antenna recently replaced, #208A, the point unit of this F-7 A-B-A set, prepares to move tonnage southward from Franklin, Missouri on July 4, 1953. The Katy obtained an average of 14,000 to 15,000 miles per 30 day month from these freight units. *(A.G. Charles)*

*(Opposite, below)* An early casuality of Katy's intensive diesel utilization program was General Electric 70-ton switcher #1651, found dead at Denison in 1953. This was the first and lightest of four similar units acquired in 1949 and 1950. Normally, branch line road-switchers, such as #1651, received scheduled maintenance and inspections on an average of every five to nine thousand miles, which was apparently inadequate in the case of this particular unit.
*(C. A. Snarrenberg)*

46

*(Left)* At 9:15 in the morning, during the summer of 1954, EMD E-8 #131 and an unknown FP-7 unit power the seven cars of the southbound BLUEBONNET, No. 27, past Tower 55 at Ft. Worth, Texas. South of this point, at Waco, Texas, a baggage car, a sleeper and a chair car were switched out and added to the San Antonio section of THE BLUEBONNET. One engine and four cars of the pictured train (baggage car, baggage mail car, baggage coach and a chair car) would travel to Houston for a 6:45 PM arrival that evening.
*(R. S. Plummer, dec., collection of Joe G. Collias)*

*(Below, left)* With silver trucks and reflective yellow and white striping, Alco PA units rivaled the original TEXAS SPECIAL E-7s in the early 50's as Katy's most colorful power. Two Alco PA-1s, led by #153A, were photographed in action at Greenville, Texas on August 17, 1953, with No. 6, the northbound KATY FLYER. On the 106 miles between Dallas and Denison, the FLYER made four stops and handled seven cars. The FLYER's name was appropriate when powered by sleek, bulbous-nosed PAs, because of their ability to rapidly accelerate after stops and to attain speeds in excess of 90 miles per hour. Management favored using the PAs for stop-and-go FLYER schedules and knew they could be counted on to make up lost time when necessary.
*(A. G. Charles)*

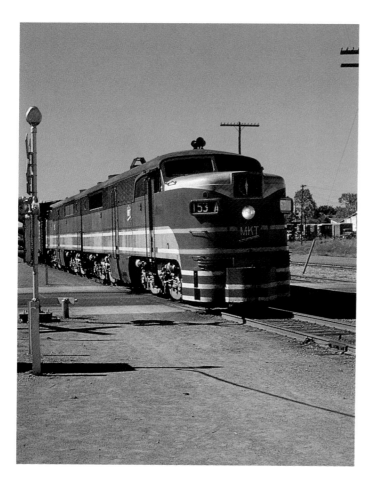

*(Opposite, above)* EMD E-8 #107A at Parsons, Kansas on May 28, 1955. At that time, MKT's nine 2250 HP E-8 units were the most common power for Katy's BLUEBONNET and the joint Katy/Frisco TEXAS SPECIAL. Maintenance schedules for these engines were fairly short, being every 5,000 miles for each unit in THE TEXAS SPECIAL pool, or after ten days of service. In 1955, the heaviest train a pair of these units was called upon to handle in normal service was the 12 cars of THE TEXAS SPECIAL between Muskogee, Oklahoma, and Denison, on the 158 mile Choctaw Subdivision. The speed limit for passenger trains on most of this route was set at 75 mph; however, this was often exceeded by the E-8s if THE TEXAS SPECIAL or BLUEBONNET was behind schedule. *(Howard Killam)*

*(Opposite, below)* Same date. A long and lank PA-2, #155C, is being readied for a turn with THE KATY FLYER at Parsons. The Katy acquired six 2000 HP PA-1s and eight 2250 HP PA-2s between 1949 and 1951, making these Alcos the most numerous mainline passenger power on the MKT. By 1955, the labor intensive paint schemes of the PAs were being simplified, with black trucks and a minimum of additional striping being the norm. *(Howard Killam)*

(Top) Each year in the 1940's and early 1950's, the Katy operated numerous special passenger movements, or extras, to events such as college football games, golf tournaments and even religious pilgrimages. One such event was a weekend trip to Columbia, Missouri from Dallas for a football game between the Southern Methodist University *Mustangs* and the Missouri University *Tigers* on September 29, 1952. On the afternoon of the contest, Mr. Don Christisen photographed the interesting assembly of equipment and power in the Katy's cramped branch line yard at Columbia. The extra was handled by EMD E-8 #132 and an unknown FP-7, carrying approximately 300 passengers, including the SMU football team and members of a booster organization. The train departed Columbia after the Saturday game at 6:30 PM for the return trip to Dallas. SMU students and boosters were scheduled to detrain at the Dallas suburban station at Highland Park, Texas, at 10:05 AM Sunday morning.

(Opposite, above) E-8 #132, carrying the white flags of an extra, and an FP-7 unit are pictured on a perfect football afternoon, a' la 1952, in the stub-ended yard at Columbia, Missouri. The view is looking northward toward the Katy depot. Also pictured are standard Pullman sleepers and Katy heavyweight cars that had been painted red and silver to blend in with, and supplement, stainless steel equipment in TEXAS SPECIAL service.

(Opposite, below) One lounge car and two diners were in the consist of the football special, including diner #437, the *Dallas*, built by ACF in 1937 and originally named the *Alamo*. The car immediately ahead of the diner appears to be the heavyweight full lounge car, *Highland Park*, painted red and silver, complete with shadow striping to simulate stainless steel fluting and silver six-wheel trucks. (All- Don M. Christisen)

M. K. & T. Depot, Columbia, Mo.

(Above) Perhaps the most picturesque branch line station on the Katy Railroad was the 1909-built brick structure at Columbia, Missouri, as seen in this early hand-tinted post card. Columbia was a thriving college town, served by both the Wabash and Katy roads. By 1951, Katy's average monthly income at Columbia was a respectable $13,670, with 653 freight cars received for the year. At that time, the principal shipper was the Dalton Coal Company, supplier of fuel to the University of Missouri's power generating station, located just south of the Katy yard. Shrinking revenues and a destructive bridge fire caused the Katy to file an abandonment application for this 9 mile branch in 1977. "The Katy Station" is now a highly successful restaurant and the old MKT right-of-way is a popular hiking and biking trail.
(D. M. Christisen collection)

50

# 1954-1956: MR. FRASER'S PROBLEM

The Katy, along with most U.S. railroads, began a difficult transition period with the closing of the Korean conflict in 1953. A 14 year Bull Market in transportation stocks, that started with the outbreak of World War II in 1939, was ending. It fell to President Donald V. Fraser to solve the problems of the Katy's past and lay plans for growth in the future, at a time when the national economy was in moderate recession. Although improvements were made to bridges and right-of-way in 1955, slow orders drastically increased because of the simultaneous deterioration of over 4 million cross ties that had been laid during World War II; many of these had been improperly treated due to war-time chemical shortages. Despite numerous difficulties and a steady drop in earnings between 1954 and 1956, management operated with a "business as usual" attitude and continued to issue dividends on Katy's cumulative preferred stock. The MKT began to abandon branch lines during this period and inaugurated piggy-back service.

*(Above)* In the summer of 1955, THE KATY FLYER, powered by Alco PA-1 #152C, nears its departure time of 11:30 AM at the MKT's downtown passenger station in Oklahoma City, Oklahoma. Noticeable in the stub-ended yard are Katy piggy-back trailers being loaded adjacent to the FLYER. The handling of trailers-on-flat-cars was inaugurated on July 6, 1954, with service initially between Kansas City, Missouri, and Oklahoma City.
*(C.A. Snarrenberg)*

*(Above)* Abandonment was less than two years away when the depot at Centerville, Kansas was photographed in 1956. Centerville was located midway between Parsons and Junction City, Kansas, on the Katy's Neosho Subdivision, which had been completed in 1870; 112 miles of this subdivision were abandoned in 1958. Larger track abandonments began in 1956, with the elimination of 48 miles of line between Mineola and Greenville, Texas. *(Howard Killam)*

*(Above)* The Katy contracted with the Coordinated Transportation Company, a wholy-owned subsidiary, for the cartage of its less than carload business, starting in 1954. By 1956, piggy-back and LCL service had been extended across the entire system. This colorful truck and trailer were photographed while on an LCL delivery in the rolling foothills of eastern Missouri, in 1956. *(S.M. Ploeger)*

*(Right)* A family snapshot of the photographer's son, young John B. Charles, "mess'n around" on the San Antonio, Texas station platform also shows a distinctive yellow MKT piggy-back trailer and several LCL trucks in the background of this view of PA-2 #154C with the northbound BLUEBONNET in June of 1955. The Katy's freight house and passenger station were in this downtown yard, while engine and car servicing and freight classification were done in nearby Sloan Yard. *(A.G. Charles)*

*(Above)* The Katy's first addition to the original 1948 set of streamlined TEXAS SPECIAL equipment came in 1954, with the purchase of replacement coach #1202R, the *J. Pinckney Henderson*, seen here at Dallas in 1964. This car was Pullman Standard's first all stainless-steel demonstrator, which seated 72 riders and cost the Katy $143,000. Although freight earnings declined in 1954, Katy's passenger, mail and express revenues increased 2.1%. President Fraser viewed the Katy's passenger service as the showpiece of the railroad and was very interested in this area of company operations. *(William J. Neill)*

*(Below)* On Thursday, March 15, 1956, ceremonies opened the new "Ultra-Modern" Katy passenger station at Garland, Texas. The station was designed by the Katy's engineering department and is considered to be the last and most modern passenger facility built by the MKT. The building's clean-cut and attractive design seemed quite fitting for this dynamic suburb of Dallas. This well-timed exposure was taken some nine years later, on the evening of June 29, 1965. *(John B. Charles)*

*The Katy Serving the Southwest*

(Above)   Among the authorized expenses for new equipment in 1955 was the purchase of an RDC-3 self-propelled unit built at the Budd Company's Red Lion, Pennsylvania plant at a cost of $170,000.  The new air-conditioned car had room for 49 passengers and included a 17 ft. baggage compartment and a 15 ft. railway post office section.   In July of 1956, RDC-3 #20 was placed in service on the 260 mile daily round trip between Denison and Wichita Falls, Texas, as Train #31 and 32.  This photo of #20 was taken at Wichita Falls, shortly before Katy passenger service to this community ended on May 16, 1959.  The RDC

was eventually traded by new management to the Chesapeake & Ohio Railroad for three hopper cars. *(Dr. Theron Baber)*

*(Below)*  As early as the mid-1920's, the Katy had used self-propelled motor cars in passenger and mail service on light density branch lines, in place of a more costly engine and standard equipment.  This painting depicts motor car #M-10 at Fayette, Missouri in 1929, where it has met southbound local No. 99.  At that time, the M-10 was making two round trips each day on the 37 mile Moberly Branch and was maintained at the Franklin, Missouri roundhouse. *(Painting by the author)*

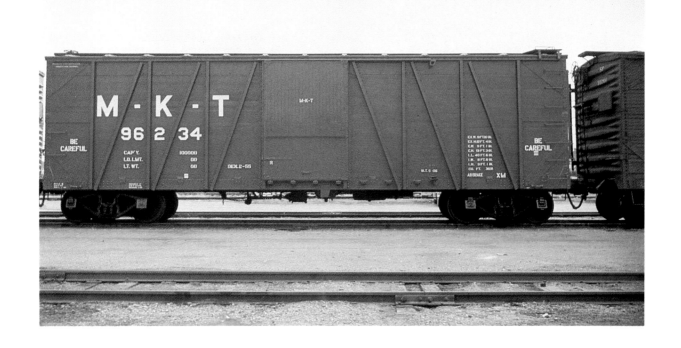

*(Above)* Box car #97627 was only several months old when photographed on January 2, 1955, off-line at Topeka, Kansas. Two hundred standard 50-ton 40'6" box cars, in the 97000-series, and three hundred 50-ton 50'6" wide-door box cars, in the 99000-series, were ordered from Pullman Standard in 1954, along with a single replacement coach, the streamlined *J. Pinckney Henderson*, at a total cost of $3,704,500. In addition, longtime Katy car builder American Car & Foundry Co. was favored with an order for 25 new 50-ton 53'6" flat cars, costing $169,610. The MKT was hard pressed to fund these necessary expenditures for new equipment. *(Howard Killam)*

*(Opposite, top)* This freshly outshopped box car looks as good as it did the day it was built in the Katy shops back in 1926. The 615 cars of the 9600-series underwent repair and/or rebuilding at the Denison, Texas car shops in 1955 and were classic examples of MKT's most basic freight equipment, of wood and outside braced construction, with steel underframes and roofs. The photograph was taken at Denison in February 1955. *(C.A. Snarrenberg)*

*(Opposite, below)* Katy bunk car #X-2059 was photographed at Ray Yard in Denison during 1954. This interesting car cannot hide its box car origins and must have given the track gangs a rough ride on those antique arch bar trucks. Bunks for 14 men were standard in these 34-foot cars. Car #X-2117, to the left, was designated as a tool car *(C.A. Snarrenberg)*

*(Above)* On September 1, 1956, there was no mistaking the Katy's depot and freight station at Paola, Kansas, due to the nicely lettered sign on top of the structure, as well as the gleaming red enameled herald on its side wall. Adding to this colorful scene were Katy work train bunk cars and a bright yellow side door caboose, #366. The caboose was used to transport passengers on the every other day mixed local between Sedalia, Missouri and Paola over the Katy's Holden Subdivision. More importantly, Paola was a key point on the Katy's mainline. In 1889 the MK&T gained trackage rights on a 43 mile section of the Ft. Scott & Memphis Railway between Paola and Kansas City, Missouri. These rights were transferred later to the Frisco Railroad and eventually to the Burlington Northern. The Paola-to-Kansas City section was an essential part of the Katy's "Short Line" from the Midwest to the Gulf ports of Houston and Galveston, Texas. *(Howard Killam)*

*(Above)* On a hot and cloudy summer's morning in 1956, an engineman ambles to his post in the cab of the leading E-7 unit, while No. 1, the southbound TEXAS SPECIAL, pauses at Waco, Texas for a crew change and the addition of cars from the Ft. Worth section of THE BLUEBONNET. By this date the once famous E-7s had lost their unique TEXAS SPECIAL lettering on their upper side panels and noses, but still wore fluted stainless steel lower side panels. This power was in obvious need of washing, which was normally done at San Antonio before returning north with No. 2. Directly behind the E-7s is a dark green Frisco RPO. *(C. A. Snarrenberg)*

*(Left)* PA-powered No. 8, left, and No. 2, right, the northbound BLUEBONNET and TEXAS SPECIAL, at the Katy's San Antonio, Texas station in June 1955. The SPECIAL was handling ten cars and departed exactly at 12:01 PM, while the BLUEBONNET left San Antonio with eight cars 30 minutes later. By the time No. 2 reached Vinita, Oklahoma, where it left Katy rails to continue on to St. Louis over the Frisco, the Kansas City bound BLUEBONNET would be a full three hours behind, due to several long stops to switch out equipment and add mail and express cars. Both trains arrived at their destinations a little after 8:00 AM the next morning. *(A.G. Charles)*

*(Opposite, above)* Enjoying breakfast aboard the Katy's streamlined dining car *Sam Houston*, in 1956, are Mr. and Mrs. C. A. Snarrenberg on their way to San Antonio on No. 1, THE TEXAS SPECIAL. *(C.A. Snarrenberg)*

*(Opposite, below)* It's a Kodak moment on the station platform at Waco, Texas, in October 1956, as Katy Southern Division superintendent R.B. George, the author's father, poses for a snapshot with his grandson John R. Forderhase and veteran TEXAS SPECIAL conductor George Tuttle. President Donald Fraser expected Katy division level officials, such as Mr. George, to look and act like top notch executives at all times. In the background is the Frisco's coach buffet-lounge, #1652 *(Mary Lee Forderhase)*

## SCHEDULE

| SOUTHBOUND | | NORTHBOUND |
|---|---|---|
| | **Frisco R. R.** | |
| Lv. 5:30 | St. Louis | Ar. 8:10 |
| Lv. 5:40 | Tower Grove | Ar. 7:50 |
| Lv. ⁶⁶5:51 | ⁶⁶Webster Groves | Ar. ⁶⁶7:37 |
| Lv. 8:01 | Newburg | Ar. 5:28 |
| Lv. 10:40 | Springfield | Ar. 2:50 |
| | **M-K-T R.R.** | |
| Ar. 2:05 | Muskogee | Lv. 11:30 |
| Ar. 3:24 | McAlester | Lv. 10:10 |
| Ar. 5:05 | Denison | Lv. 8:35 |
| Ar. 6:19 | Greenville | Lv. 7:16 |
| Ar. 7:18 | ⁶⁶Highland Park | Lv. 6:18 |
| Ar. 7:30 | Dallas | Lv. 6:10 |
| Lv. 7:45 | Union Station | Ar. 5:55 |
| Ar. 7:35 | Fort Worth | Lv. 5:10 |
| Ar. a10:05 | Wichita Falls | Lv. b4:10 |
| Ar. 9:40 | Waco | Lv. 4:00 |
| Ar. 11:59 | Austin | Lv. 1:42 |
| Ar. 1:55 | San Antonio | Lv. 12:01 |

a Change at Denison to Train 31.
b Train 32 from Wichita Falls arrives Denison 7:50 pm connecting with Train 2.
⁶⁶No baggage checked to or from this station.
⁶⁶Stops on signal to pick up revenue passengers for Oklahoma and Texas.
⁶⁶Stops to let off revenue passengers from Texas and Oklahoma.
am times light type—**pm times bold type.**

## MISSOURI · KANSAS · OKLAHOMA · TEXAS

# 1957-1965: THE EVE OF DESTRUCTION

On January 8, 1957, the Katy's Board of Directors, led by Robert E. Thomas, elected William N. Deramus, III, president of the M-K-T and moved Donald Fraser to the post of Chairman of the Board. Sweeping changes were initiated by Mr. Thomas and the Board, prompted by the steady decline of Katy's fortunes starting in 1954. With the full approval of the Board, Mr. Deramus immediately began the wholesale transformation of the Katy, including a drastic reduction in the work force and the elimination of any unprofitable or marginal operation. Entire departments disappeared overnight, as thousands of jobs were terminated; this caused a sudden decline in service to shippers, which ironically lost business for the Katy. Deramus' inability to clearly articulate the reasons why the changes were necessary seriously affected employee morale and contributed to the prevailing belief among the rail community that the Katy Railroad would soon be out of business; it narrowly survived.

*(Above)* On September 1, 1957, southbound No. 5, THE KATY FLYER, has stopped at Nevada, Missouri on its route between St. Louis and Parsons, Kansas. The single PA-2, #155C, was handling its normal five cars, plus an extra head end car and a business car on the rear. The mail storage car, immediately behind #155C, was one of ten ex-Pullman tourist sleepers, converted in the Katy's Denison car shops in 1956. In exactly eight months, on May 1, 1958, this section of THE KATY FLYER would be abolished as a cost savings measure by the Deramus administration. *(Thomas R. Lee)*

*(Opposite page, top)* The arrival of No. 2, THE TEXAS SPECIAL, in St. Louis, Missouri, at 8:00 AM on the morning of September 12, 1958, was indeed something special because of the use of run-through Katy power on the Frisco leg of the route. The lead unit, E-8 #135, wears its original number and paint scheme while its trailing mate is in freshly painted Deramus colors, sporting a newly assigned number. By the end of 1960, the entire Katy diesel roster would be renumbered.
*(Walter E. Zullig, Jr.)*

*(Opposite page, bottom)* By August of 1958, the elaborate Victorian-era passenger station at Ft. Scott, Kansas had been closed, due to the abandonment of passenger service on the Sedalia and St. Louis Sub-divisions, effective May 1 of that year. To avoid continued tax expenses, this seventy-year-old facility was demolished in 1959. *(Emery Gulash)*

*(Above)* Consistent with William Deramus, III's, plan to rebuild the Katy into a model of efficiency and modernization was the creation of a streamlined version of the famous Katy corporate emblem in 1957. The new herald soon became a symbolic reminder of hard economic times for the Katy Railroad. *(John B. Charles)*

*(Above)* Freshly painted EMD GP-7 #101 (originally #1511) glistens in the sunshine at the Katy's engine facility at Wichita Falls, Texas, on a chilly January day in 1959. Gone are the Fraser era diagonal yellow warning stripes, along with the jobs of the skilled craftsmen who painted them, the result of heavy layoffs in the Katy's mechanical department during 1957 and 1958. By 1959, four thousand jobs had been cut systemwide. Bad order locomotives, or those units requiring major repairs, had risen from 3.7% of the total power fleet in 1956 to an amazing 34.6% by 1958. Mr. Deramus gave the rebuilding of Katy's diesel power top priority throughout most of his four years as president; however, his program to simplify and modernize was hindered from the outset by the continued decline of operating revenues. *(Dr. Theron Baber)*

*(Right)* By 1961, the predominatly red paint scheme of the early Deramus years had given way to a slight variation, with black pilots on all passenger and freight units. FP-7 #78C, formerly #121C, is on the point of an eastbound manifest freight at Spanish Lake, Missouri, just moments away from its St. Louis Baden Yard destination, during October 1961. *(Mel Nierdieck)*

*(Opposite, above)* In October 1958, THE TEXAS SPECIAL, No. 2, has arrived at Union Station at St. Louis, Missouri, behind newly painted Katy FP-7 units, with #122C in the lead. In a few months, on January 4, 1959, the MKT's agreement with the Frisco Railroad for the joint operation of the SPECIAL was terminated and Katy passenger service to St. Louis became a historical footnote. *(Mel Nierdieck)*

*(Opposite, below)* On January 12, 1959, the same #122C, still wearing its original engine number, was found at Wichita Falls, Texas with Train No. 32. This train was scheduled to depart Wichita Falls Union Station at 4:20 PM daily for a four hour trip to the Katy division point at Denison, Texas. Track conditions on the Katy's 105 mile Henrietta Subdivision were such that a considerable amount of mud was sprayed upon the sides of #122C, later renumbered 79C.
*(Dr. Theron Baber)*

## CLASSIFICATION OF ENGINES

| CLASS | UNITS | ENGINE NUMBERS | Equipped For MU Control | Geared For Maximum Speed |
|---|---|---|---|---|
| D-1 | 4 | 1651 to 1654 incl. | No | 55 |
| D-2 | 2 | 101 A-C | Yes | 85 |
| D-3 | 4 | 106 A-C & 107 A-C | Yes | 85 |
|  | 5 | 131 to 135 incl. | Yes | 85 |
| D-4 | 14 | 151 A-C to 157 A-C incl. | Yes | 90 |
| D-5 | 6 | 1 to 6 incl. | Yes | 65 |
|  | 11 | 1000 to 1010 incl. | No | 60 |
|  | 5 | 1026 to 1030 incl. | No | 60 |
|  | 15 | 1201 to 1215 incl. | No | 60 |
|  | 10 | 1226 to 1235 incl. | No | 65 |
| D-6 | 12 | 121 A-B-C to 124 A-B-C incl. | Yes | 77 |
| D-7 | 20 | 201 A-B-C to 207 A-B incl. | Yes | 65 |
|  | 12 | 208 A-B-C to 211 A-B-C incl. | Yes | 65 |
|  | 12 | 226 A-B-C to 229 A-B-C incl. | Yes | 65 |
|  | 18 | 326 A-C to 334 A-C incl. | Yes | 65 |
| D-8 | 29 | 1501 to 1529 incl. | Yes | 65 |
|  | 2 | 1701, 1702 | Yes | 80 |
|  | 4 | 1731 to 1734 incl. | Yes | 80 |
| D-9 | 13 | 1551 to 1563 incl. | Yes | 65 |
|  | 16 | 1571 to 1586 incl. | Yes | 70 |
|  | 1 | 1591 | No | 70 |
|  | 2 | 1787, 1788 | Yes | 70 |
| Total | 221 | | | |

## WEIGHT OF EMPTY PASSENGER CARS

| Class | Numbers | | Length In Feet | Tons |
|---|---|---|---|---|
| Baggage | 173, 175, 177-179, | | | |
|  | 181-185, 187-189, 191 | | 73 | 69 |
|  | 2650-2655, 2657-2664 | | 73 | 69 |
|  | 216-217 | | 64 | 63 |
|  | 235 | | 74 | 68 |
|  | 252-254 | | 73 | 69 |
| Baggage-Mail | 218-224, 226-234 | | 74 | 68 |
|  | 1000 | | 73 | 55 |
| Mail | 30, 2900, 2901 | | 64 | 66 |
| Mail-Storage | 50 | | 64 | 60 |
|  | 201-209 | | 81 | 68 |
| Chair | 901-913, 915-925 | AC | 81 | 81 |
|  | 1200, 1201 | AC | 85 | 63 |
|  | 1202-R | AC | 85 | 66 |
|  | 1203-1207 | AC | 85 | 68 |
| Coach | 641-645 | AC | 81 | 90 |
| Chair-Lounge-Buffet | 1300, 1301 | AC | 85 | 66 |
| Lounge | 494, 495 | AC | 82 | 91 |
|  | 496 | AC | 82 | 83 |
| Diner | 437-438, 2050 | AC | 81 | 92 |
|  | 1100 | AC | 85 | 68 |
|  | 1110 | AC | 85 | 75 |
| Sleeper | 1500-1506 | AC | 85 | 70 |
|  | (Clover) Glade, | | | |
|  | Meadow, Brook | AC | 84 | 93 |
|  | Keightley | AC | 82 | 86 |
|  | Lake Jessie | AC | 83 | 89 |
|  | McCallsburg | AC | 83 | 88 |
|  | Kimbell | AC | 83 | 87 |
|  | McInnis | AC | 83 | 88 |
|  | McKeever | AC | 83 | 87 |
|  | McMasterville | AC | 83 | 87 |
|  | Parsons | AC | 82 | 86 |
|  | San Antonio | AC | 82 | 86 |
|  | Sunnyside | AC | 83 | 88 |
|  | Whitehead | AC | 82 | 88 |
| Observation-Lounge-Sleeper | 1100 | AC | 85 | 68 |
| Business Car | 100 | AC | 81 | 101 |
| " | 401 | AC | 82 | 99 |
| " | 103 | AC | 80 | 98 |

*(Above)* This classification of engines and a weight table for all 135 Katy passenger cars was on page 16 of the M-K-T Lines' Time Table No. 30, effective as of July 20, 1958.

(Above) A good example of the Deramus motive power program was engine #32, shown in action at Kansas City, Kansas in 1960. This Baldwin model DS44-1000 was one of the Katy's earliest diesel switchers, having been built in 1947. Between 1957 and 1960, Katy's eleven DS44-1000s, numbered 1000-1010, were repowered with EMD 1000 HP 12 cylinder 567C engines and renumbered 22-32; they also received new EMD long hoods. All but three of these veteran workhorses survived until their final dispositions in 1986-87. (Howard Killam)

(Opposite page, top) Katy's #1235, an SW-9 built by EMD in 1952, still wears its original number and paint scheme in this view taken at Dallas Yard in August 1959. This switcher was soon renumbered 21 and later rebuilt by EMD in 1961, along with three other SW-9s, again as a 1200 HP unit. While yards at St. Louis, Missouri, Parsons, Kansas, Denison and Bellmead, Texas were being rearranged and modernized during 1959, the facilities at smaller yards, such as Dallas, were showing signs of neglect. (John B. Charles)

(Opposite page, bottom) General Electric 70-tonner #1653 was found in the Katy's North Yard in Wichita Falls, Texas, on January 4, 1959. Due to the limited amount of work Katy's four GEs could handle, and their necessary, yet costly, parts inventory, management decided to drop these units from the roster as each engine came due for major servicing. By the end of April 1959, all 4 units had been sold to Bugbee Railway Equipment Company of San Antonio, Texas. These were the first of Katy's original diesels to be disposed of and were never included in the new renumbering program. (Dr. Theron Baber)

(Above, right) In August 1959, an early cab unit, EMD F-3 #203A awaits its next assignment at Dallas, Texas. This 1500 HP F-3 had been built in June 1947 and was eventually designated as #67A in the 1960 renumbering. By the end of 1959, bad order locomotives had been decreased to 29% of the fleet (64 engines). Unfortunately, the Katy experienced a marked decline in the shipment of agricultural products and general traffic during that year because of a poor wheat harvest and a national steel strike. (John B. Charles)

65

*(Above)* It's almost noon on September 9, 1959, at the MKT's Denison passenger station, built in 1912 and representative of traditional neoclassical architectural design. In the foreground of the scene, and quite fitting, is another classic: a 1957 Chevy *Belair* coupe, the identifying emblem for a generation of Americans born after World War II who grew up with black and white television, "Golden Age" rock 'n' roll and numerous medium-sized railroads such as the Katy. After January 1, 1959, all train dispatching for the entire 2,918 mile Katy Railroad was handled from the Denison office, located on the second floor of this station. This was another characteristic cost saving measure by President Deramus that eventually helped the Katy become more responsive to the needs of shippers and more accountable to top management. *(John B. Charles)*

*(Above)* This streetside view of the Denison station, from a postcard, gives a glimpse of the beautiful park and fountain that greeted travelers prior to 1959. With the consolidation and relocation of many departments to new quarters in the Denison passenger station in the late 1950's, there came a desperate need for additional parking. The decision was made to quickly bulldoze the fountain and park in front of the station and spread a layer of gravel for a new parking lot. The Katy used the building as its operating headquarters until 1983, when more modern facilities were acquired. The now privately owned station and lovely park have both been restored to their former splendor and an excellent railroad museum is located on the first floor.
*(B. Allen Young Collection)*

*(Opposite, above)* At Wichita Falls, Texas, No. 31 has just arrived on a cool February morning in 1959 from its 130 mile trip from Denison, where it had departed at 6:15 AM. This was a TEXAS SPECIAL connection that carried passengers who arrived on No. 1 at Denison at 5:30 AM, on to Wichita Falls and the communities on the Henrietta Subdivision. In the consist was a single baggage RPO and one of Katy's very comfortable 900-series chair cars, #910, built by ACF in 1938. These modern heavyweights had adjustable tilt seats that could be swung around to face the windows, as well as fold-away tables, air conditioning and diffused lighting. *(Dr. Theron A. Baber)*

*(Opposite, below)* On the afternoon of February 8, 1959, Train No. 32 was ready for the highball from Wichita Falls Union Station for the run to Denison and its connection with the northbound TEXAS SPECIAL that evening. No. 32 normally consisted of the Budd RDC-3 #20; however, due to servicing requirements, an EMD FP-7, #124C, and its two car consist were in use that day. MKT passenger service to Wichita Falls ended in several months, on May 16, 1959, immediately following the approval of Katy's application for discontinuance before the Texas Railroad Commission. *(Dr. Theron A. Baber)*

(Above)   This unique view of the Katy's Dallas Yard was taken from atop the signal bridge at the southern end of the yard by a very energetic Bill Neill on January 24, 1964. Manifest freight No. 41 has arrived from its morning run over the Dallas Subdivision from Denison behind EMD F-3 #70A and three other units.  Dallas Yard had a capacity of 438 cars in 1956 and included diesel servicing and car repair facilities at the upper left.  In addition to the eight-story Katy Building in downtown Dallas, considered an archetectural gem, a large freight station and a seven-story warehouse were adjacent to Dallas Yard.  Gross station earnings at Dallas in 1964 were $18 million, compared to over $19 million in 1955 .

(Below)   As a result of a severe motive power availability problem starting in 1958, the Katy leased power from the Kansas City Southern, Wabash, Chicago Great Western and even the Pennsylvania.  Chicago Great Western #102-C was photographed at Dallas, Texas on a cool February morning in 1962.  In addition to necessary leased power, President Deramus initiated longer and heavier trains, as a means of reducing train miles.  Local freight trains were eliminated on most subdivisions, which meant industry and local switching had to be done often with trains of 150 or more cars;  a trainman's nightmare!
*(Above- William J. Neill, below- John B. Charles)*

(Above)  Among the most successful results of Mr. Deramus' program to rebuild Katy road power was engine #128, originally an AS-16 built by Baldwin in 1950, pictured at Dallas Yard in October 1961.  All but one of Katy's eighteen AS-16s were rebuilt by EMD between 1958 and 1960 with dependable 1500 HP sixteen cylinder 567C engines.  The most noticeable change was the replacement of their long hoods with EMD GP-9 style hoods.  Their first generation numbers of 1787 and 1571-1586 became #124-141 respectively in the 1960 renumbering.  Boiler-equipped #1788 was assigned #125, but was never re-engined and became the first of these roadswitchers to be disposed of in 1969.

(Below)  Fresh from the Katy paint shop in September 1964 is former Alco RS-3 #1559, renumbered 152 and repowered in 1960 with an EMD 1500 HP prime mover. Katy modified only six of its original fifteen RS-3s:  #1701 and 1702 (two boiler-equipped dual-service units), 1553 and 1559-1561.  These engines received new numbers 142, 143, 146 and 152-154 respectively.  For the next 28 years the RS-3Ms were used primarily for heavy yard chores at Parsons, Kansas, Denison and Bellmead, Texas;  however, they also were utilized as road power when needed.
*(Above- John B. Charles, below- Dr. Tom Hughes)*

| FOURTH CLASS | | TIMETABLE No. 29 | | FOURTH CLASS |
|---|---|---|---|---|
| **51** Way | Distance from St. Louis | EFFECTIVE 12:01 A.M. March 1, 1957 | Symbols and Capacity of Sidings | **50** Way |
| Daily Except Sunday | | **STATIONS** | | Daily Except Sunday |
| AM 5.00 | | N **RAY** RA | WGTSYP Yard | PM 1.00 |
| 5.25 | 662.5 | **SUN** 3.6 | P    NS | 12.40 |
| 5.40 | 666.1 | **ELLSWORTH** 5.5 | 20 | 12.25 |
| AM 6.05 | 671.6 | T&P Crossing-Gate D **SHERMAN** SN 9.1 | S Yard | PM 12.01 |
| **51** | | | | **50** |
| 8.4 | | Average speed per hour | | 9.1 |

**SHERMAN SUBDIVISION**
SOUTHWARD                    NORTHWARD

NO. 51 IS SUPERIOR TO NO. 50

*(Opposite, above)* Alco RS-3 #148, formerly #1556, was stationed at Denison's Ray Yard in the autumn of 1963 for use on the nine mile branch line south to Sherman, Texas, county seat of Grayson County. By 1968, all but the six modified, or "morphodite," RS-3Ms would be removed from the roster through either trade-in to EMD or sale to salvage dealers.

*(Opposite, below)* On the afternoon of October 8, 1963, RS-3 #148 is returning to Denison from a day of interchange and local work in Sherman. In the background are the well kept fairways of the Katy Employees' Golf Course. *(Both photos- Earl Holloway)*

*(Above, top)* Katy's first generation power was a representative cross section of most U.S. builders, including five H16-44s built in 1950-51 by the Fairbanks-Morse Company of Beloit, Wisconsin. Original numbers were 1591 and 1731-1734, with these renumbered 157-161 respectively in 1960. Although early 1950's color coverage is lacking, these Deramus-era in-service views are included which are themselves quite rare, due to the tendency of these units to be on the repair tracks waiting for the arrival of necessary parts. The first unit, #1591, was built for general purpose use only, while the remaining four engines (#1731-1734) arrived in 1951 equipped with steam boilers for use as back-up mainline passenger power, notably on the Houston section of THE BLUEBONNET and for THE TEXAS SPECIAL connection to and from Wichita Falls, Texas. Mr. Deramus' mechanical department recommended all five FM units merited overhauling as freight-only units and returned these to Fairbanks-Morse in 1959-60 to be re-engined. No. 161 was photographed at Dallas Yard on November 22, 1962. *(John B. Charles)*

*(Above, right)* FM H16-44 #159 was teamed up with EMD SW-1200 #6 as the second trick switcher at Denison's Ray Yard in April 1964. *(Dr. Tom Hughes)*

*(Above)* On the morning of September 12, 1963, manifest freight No. 41 is at the southeastern edge of Denison, Texas, traversing the 90-pound rail of the Dallas Subdivision. This was a daily Kansas City-to-Houston train that paused in Dallas to deliver cars and add southbound tonnage to its consist. Just a moment earlier, these engines passed the birthplace and early home of Dwight D. Eisenhower, 34th President of the United States. It is a little known fact that President Eisenhower's father worked for the Katy at Denison, prior to moving his young family to Abilene, Kansas. Power for No. 41 was provided by well-groomed FP-7 #80C, plus two F-3 boosters and another A unit. *(Earl Holloway)*

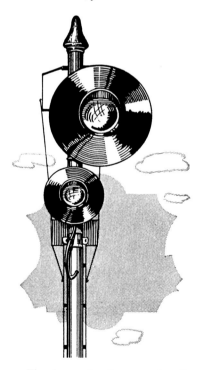

The above artwork was used on the contents page of each bi-monthly *Katy Employes' Magazine,* which was the first item to be terminated by Mr. Deramus upon his arrival in January 1957. *(George Collection)*

*(Above)* This colorful Katy turtleback RPO was in the consist of No. 6, the northbound KATY FLYER, at Denison in March 1964. As a cost savings move in the late 1950's, the Katy ceased making major repairs to its passenger car fleet by selling a portion of its heavyweight dining, baggage and postal cars to the Darby Corporation of Kansas City, Kansas. Darby then rebuilt or repaired the cars and leased them back to the Katy. Among the modifications made to RPO #32, built in 1916 by ACF, was the replacement of the original clerestory roof and the alteration of its side windows. Most noticeable was this car's bright new red paint job and the simplified company moniker "KATY" in yellow letters above the windows. *(Dr. Tom Hughes)*

*(Above)* On August 11, 1963 modified FA-1 #89C was at the Kansas City roundhouse in the company of EMD F-3 A and B units. Because new power could not be afforded, the MKT had re-engined each of its eighteen Alco FA units starting in the summer of 1956 with FA-1s #326A and #326C, rebuilt at LaGrange with EMD prime movers. Two other FA-1s, #329A and #329C, were repowered by Alco in 1956 and later renumbered 85A and 85C; these two anomalies remained in service as Katy's only 100% Alco cab units, until their trade-in to EMD in 1967. With no other exceptions, the remaining fifteen FA-1s and replacement unit, FA-2 #87A, were repowered with EMD 1500 HP 16 cylinder 567C

engines by the close of 1959. By then, all fourteen Alco PA-1 and PA-2 passenger units had been pushed onto storage tracks to wait for final disposition.

*(Below)* Modified Alco FA-1 #89A was being hostled near the Parsons, Kansas locomotive shops on January 3, 1963. To the unitiated Katy observer, little change is apparent in this unit's new appearance other than the hump on its roof line, necessitated by its EMD 567C prime mover. Included in the modifications was the placement of multiple unit cable sockets above the headlight, which gave the Katy's revised FAs a somewhat hog-like profile. *(Both- Dr. Louis A. Marre)*

*(Above)* In heavy action at Kellogg, Texas during December 1963 is wrecker #X-255, nicknamed "The Big Hook." This was Katy's first 250-ton diesel wrecker, built in 1957 by Industrial Brownhoist. As a result of insufficient revenues and the emphasis on rebuilding Katy's power fleet between 1957 and 1964, track and roadbed maintenance were deferred except where it was deemed absolutely essential. During the four years of the Deramus presidency, the Katy reduced maintenance-of-way expenditures by almost half the amount invested during the previous four years of the Fraser administration. The consequences of this policy were disastrous; by 1964 the Katy was plagued by an average of 20 derailments a month!

*(Below)* The wrecker outfit train is moving northward near Waxahachie, Texas, on its return trip to Denison, where #X-255 was headquartered. Because of the increasing number of derailments and the need to clear the mainline quickly, management adopted the practice of bulldozing derailed cars off the tracks rather than incurring the cost of using wreckers to rerail cars. If a derailment occurred near a highway, a junk dealer was usually called in to cut up the cars. If derailed cars were inaccessible to a highway, they were simply left where they had been pushed off the tracks. By 1965, over 300 wrecked cars were scattered along the Katy's right-of-way. This photo was taken in 1966, during slightly better times. *(Both photos- John B. Charles)*

(Above) The engineer of southbound train No. 53 is poised for a train order pickup at Durant, Oklahoma during the early evening of September 17, 1963; power was provided by EMD GP-7s #113 and #107. At Durant, the Katy crossed an east-west line of the Frisco Railroad and shared a handsome brick passenger station with that company. A change in station operations came on May 1, 1964, when an agreement was signed with the Missouri Pacific Railroad that granted the MP trackage rights on the Katy's 44-mile line between Durant and Whitesboro, Texas. (Earl Holloway)

(Below) A plume of black exhaust from FP-7 #74A pours into the air, as that unit and an unknown roadswitcher struggle with the tonnage of a southbound train at Itasca, Texas, in March of 1965. Itasca was located on the Katy's Ft. Worth Subdivision, 42 miles north of Bellmead, Texas, this train's destination and crew change point. The Itasca depot appears deserted and track conditions look to be poor; however, as with almost all things on the Katy, looks were deceiving. This station was in fact an open agency that earned $84,508 in gross revenues in 1965. Although the mainline was in obvious need of major ballasting, the rail in this photo was some of Katy's best at that time, being 115 lb., laid new in 1950. (Dr. Tom Hughes)

On November 1, 1961, the M-K-T's Board of Directors accepted the resignation of William Deramus, III, and appointed Charles T. Williams President of the Katy. Mr. Williams was a 27 year veteran of Katy service, having been Vice President and General Manager since 1955. Only minor changes in operating procedures and personnel occurred during the Williams presidency from 1961 to 1965, chiefly because the Katy's Board of Directors remained firmly in the control of Robert E. Thomas, who had brought Mr. Deramus to the Katy in 1957. The Board was virtually in a panic over the Katy's worsening financial condition and recommended further expense reductions, as well as a continuation of the Deramus prescription of service and maintenance curtailments.

Mr. Williams initiated the drastic policy of not allowing any repair on the railroad that would incur even a minor expense without his personal approval. Eventually, two costly locomotive fires were caused by lack of proper maintenance and repair restrictions. By 1964, when the Katy suffered an $8.5 million deficit, schedules had been reduced to one train per day to and from the major terminals. As an expense reduction, hot water was cut off in lavatories and wash rooms. At that low point, the Katy was handling an average of only 500 loaded cars per day and oil companies were refusing to deliver engine fuel, unless paid in advance.

*(Left)* A craftsman in the Denison car shops carefully touches up the number on new bay-window road caboose #68 in November 1961. Between June 1959 and January 1962, the Katy constructed ten cabooses, numbered 60-69, using steel underframes from earlier cabooses in the 751-795 series. These new way cars were Katy's only bay-window cabooses. The Denison, shops were closed for extended periods in 1961; despite this, car department forces did manage to make running and classified repairs to 422 freight cars and 6 passenger cars. *(John B. Charles)*

*(Left)* The Katy continued to acquire new freight equipment during the Deramus and Williams regimes by way of long-term lease, rather than through standard plans for installment purchase requiring a 20% down payment. In 1964 the MKT received car #1427 as part of an order of 49 non-insulated cushion underframe 77-ton capacity box cars. This car was photographed at Kansas City, Missouri in August 1964. At the beginning of 1965, Katy's freight car ownership totaled 9,966 cars, but 21% of these were in bad order.
*(Fred Lyon, dec., University of Missouri-Columbia / Western Manuscripts Collection)*

(Above)  The most extensive Deramus/Williams maintenance-of-way projects were line revisions in central Oklahoma between 1960 and 1963, necessitated by the construction of two government financed dams and reservoirs, one at Osage, the other at Eufaula, Oklahoma.  The project at Osage relocated and rebuilt over six miles of mainline on the Parsons, Kansas-to-Oklahoma City, Oklahoma line, in connection with the construction of Keystone Dam and Reservoir.  Over eleven miles were rebuilt in the vicinity of Eufaula, on the Katy's mainline between Muskogee, Oklahoma and Denison, Texas, due to the construction of Eufaula Dam and its huge reservoir.  The mechanized tie gang is working on the mainline in front of the Eufaula depot on the afternoon of September 27, 1963, causing southbound No. 5, THE KATY FLYER, to use the adjacent siding during its station stop.  By that date, No. 5 consisted of a single coach , an RPO, two baggage cars and a Santa Fe express box car.  The Santa Fe car was added to No. 5 each morning at Kansas City from ATSF No. 7, for Chicago-to-Dallas express mail.  Power was supplied that day by EMD E-8 #56A and an unidentified FP-7.  (Earl Holloway)

(Right)  Probably the most recognizable way cars on the Katy roster were a group of 25 outside braced single sheathed cabooses in the 796-820 series. These "crummies" had been built in the Denison car shops in 1930;  all were reconditioned in 1957-1959, again at Denison, and renumbered 31-53.

At Dallas Yard on March 6, 1965, caboose #37 was wearing the faded livery of the Deramus presidency.  Although it appears more suited to lazy transfer chores, #37 had been modernized and was outfitted for road duty with two-way radio and roller bearing trucks.
(William J. Neill)

*(Above)* Northbound No. 6, THE KATY FLYER, has just made a station stop at Durant, Oklahoma on a crisp and beautiful January 16, 1964, and is again underway with its five car train. The insulated express car immediately behind the power protected a shipment of Rio Grande Valley produce from the subfreezing temperatures. On the point of this good looking train, ahead of an unknown F-7 B unit, was big E-8 #53C. *(Earl Holloway)*

*(Left)* The time is the afternoon of March 6, 1965, on the yard tracks of Dallas Union Terminal and, as the old television show always stated, "YOU ARE THERE," in the cab of EMD E-8 #53C as it is being hostled over to Union Station from the Katy's nearby Dallas Yard. No. 53C will be readied for its 9:00 PM departure that evening with No. 2, THE TEXAS SPECIAL. The cement railing to the left was for the infamous Elm Street underpass, at Dealey Plaza, where our youngest elected United States President, John F. Kennedy, was shot and assassinated on November 22, 1963.

As was often the case, a Katy business car was parked adjacent to that same underpass on the day of the assassination. Immediately after the shooting, the business car was mistakenly thought to have been used by the assassin and was thoroughly searched by Secret Service agents. A Katy valet on board the car was somewhat shaken by these events, especially after being closely questioned by the anxious agents.
*(William J. Neill)*

*(Above)* A crewman of No. 5, the southbound KATY FLYER, has his arm raised for a train order pickup at the Katy's interlocking tower immediately south of the Muskogee, Oklahoma passenger station, on October 19, 1963. Katy operators manned this tower continuously to protect the mainline at this point from movements of the intersecting Frisco and Midland Valley roads. The addition of a single Missouri Pacific baggage car to No. 5's standard five car consist indicates the MP did not make its normal connection with No. 1, THE TEXAS SPECIAL, the previous evening in Kansas City. In the early 1960's, the Missouri Pacific contracted to transfer a Kansas City-to-San Antonio express mail car from its Train No. 15, after arrival from St. Louis each evening in K.C., to the Katy's No. 1 before the departure time of 10:00 PM. Obviously, this day it was necessary to add the car to No. 5, which was highballed out of Kansas City's Union Station at 8:25 AM that morning. *(Earl Holloway)*

*(Below)* The train order board is in the up position, as No. 5's fireman snags the headend's set of flimsies at Hunt, Texas, on the outskirts of Greenville, in May 1962. Of particular interest is the red Katy caboose on the tail of No. 5, which was being deadheaded to a southern destination. As the rule book specified, the Katy operator has posted himself in a good position to get a clear view of the train. If any problem is noticed during No. 5's passage, word will immediately be radioed to the crew. *(John B. Charles)*

*(Above)* This public timetable was in effect during the last year of Katy passenger service. *(George Collection)*

(Below) Katy passenger service was on the verge of extinction when full dining car #1100, the *Sam Houston*, was photographed at Denison, on September 6, 1964. On July 26, 1964, service south of Dallas to San Antonio had been discontinued because of the loss of a "million dollar" mail contract to a trucking firm. After that date, abbreviated versions of THE TEXAS SPECIAL and KATY FLYER continued to operate only between Kansas City and Dallas; however, neither train carried a full diner. The shortened SPECIAL, Nos. 1 and 2, consisted of two baggage RPOs and a baggage-express car, one coach, one coach-buffet-lounge and a single sleeper.

Despite the hard times, the *Sam Houston*, still exuded a certain glamour, having been Katy's only stainless-steel streamlined diner, built by Pullman Standard in 1948. Its original red roof and silver trucks were later simplified to black, but those flashy side panels remained. This historic car was sold to the Spokane, Portland & Seattle in 1966. (Earl Holloway)

*Several eras of Katy dining car service are represented in this collection of Katy china, glass and silverware. From the 1931-1948 period is the water bottle in the foreground, as well as the silver teapot, creamer and sugar bowl. The three pieces of china were from the last decade of dining car service, 1955-1965, and were purchased by an employee from the company after passenger service ended on June 30, 1965. San Antonio's famous Alamo, symbol of Texas liberty, was pictured on the simple yet elegant dinner plate, used exclusively on THE TEXAS SPECIAL. From the Deramus period are the luncheon menu and note card. The beverage glass and silver dinnerware were in use from 1945-1965. (R. George photo)*

(Above) EMD F-3 #65A leads its northbound train and a parade of power past Tower 55, in downtown Ft. Worth, Texas, on a cloudless June morning in 1964. This train's caboose has just cleared the yard limits of the Katy's Ney Yard, 1.4 miles south of the tower, listed in Katy time-tables of that period as, "T.&P. (Texas & Pacific) Crossing." A century ago, Tower 55 received its well known number from the newly formed Texas Railroad Commission, which number-ed towers in the *Lone Star State* in chronological order based on the date of their con-struction. Between Ft. Worth and Whitesboro, Texas, the Katy utilized 72 miles of trackage rights on the Miss-ouri Pacific-controlled T.&P. This track was used jointly since 1881, when the infam-ous rail manipulator Jay Gould controlled the three railroads simultaneously. As a result of government dereg-ulation in the 1980's, these three roads were brought together again, by way of merger, under the banner of the Union Pacific Railroad. *(Dr. Tom Hughes)*

(Below) The Dallas skyline was still in the formative stage when Business Car #401 was photographed on its storage track adjacent to the Union Terminal on June 26, 1964. This beautiful car had been construced at the Sedalia, Missouri car shops in 1949 from the body and underframe of the heavyweight diner *James Bowie*, built originally by ACF in 1931. It was a Katy tradition to provide this car for the use of its Vice President of Operations, at that time Mr. T.S. Carter. Only seven months earlier, the course of world events was changed when shots were fired from the Texas School Book Depository in the near background. *(William J. Neill)*

**NATURAL ROUTE SOUTHWEST**

81

# 1965-1970: "COUNT ON KATY!"

John Walker Barriger, III, was at the end of an illustrious railroading career when he was asked to accept the post as Katy's chief executive on March 11, 1965. Barriger viewed the job with the Missouri-Kansas-Texas as an opportunity to put many of his favorite theories on successful railroading into actual practice. The major problems were identified in the spring of 1965 and four lines of attack initiated to bring about the Katy's recovery: (1) Extensive development of fixed property and equipment; (2) Improved freight service; (3) Intensified sales efforts; and (4) Revitalized morale. From the outset, President Barriger realized the formation of a few very large western rail systems was inevitable and began the search for a suitable merger partner for the Katy. As advertised by the phrase he coined, Mr. Barriger's tireless efforts convinced shippers they could *COUNT ON KATY* once again.

*(Above)* Mr. Barriger understood the effectiveness of images in advertising and restored the famous MISS KATY, used originally in the 1890's, as the symbol of the revitalized M-K-T Railroad of the 1960's, outfitted accordingly in a trendy "mod" mini-skirt and boots. *(George Collection)*

*(Above)* Number 400, the private business car of the MKT's new president, John W. Barriger, III, was on the tail of No. 2, the northbound TEXAS SPECIAL at Dallas on the evening of June 26, 1965.

*(Opposite page, top)* Same date. Power for THE TEXAS SPECIAL was provided by modified E-8 #52C on that warm shirt sleeve evening. In only four days, all Katy passenger service ended as a result of declining ridership and the continued loss of postal contracts to low-bidding trucking companies. John Barriger saw no advantages for the Katy in continuing its passenger service and agreed with previous management's decision to become a freight-only carrier. At the time, every dollar of revenue was desperately needed to fund the new program for recovery.

*(Opposite page, bottom)* At Dallas Union Terminal, Train No. 1, the southbound TEXAS SPECIAL has just completed its last run on the morning of July 1, 1965. KATY FLYER service had ceased with the arrival of the last No. 5 at Dallas the previous evening. The cost of passenger service on the Katy Railroad could no longer be afforded. *(All- John B. Charles)*

(Above) On the afternoon of June 24, 1965, with only six days of life remaining, No. 5, the southbound KATY FLYER has stopped at Muskogee, Oklahoma on its run between Kansas City and Dallas. Muskogee was the scheduled meeting and crew change point for daylight Trains #5 and 6, as well as the nighttime runs of Nos. 1 and 2, THE TEXAS SPECIAL. Although Katy passenger service was at its end, E-8 #55A appeared to be the very picture of good maintenance on that day and still drew admiring looks from the local citizenry. Muskogee was, and remains today, the headquarters for the Five Civilized Tribes of Oklahoma; early in the 19th century, each tribe had been assigned a segment of the original Indian Territory. *(John B. Charles)*

(Below) The Katy's large Romanesque-style station was an important landmark in downtown Muskogee during the passenger service era. Such an extensive facility was needed to house the dispatching and clerical staff for the superintendent of the M-K-T's Southern District, which included 275 miles of mainline between Parsons, Kansas and Denison, Texas, as well as the 80 mile Tulsa Subdivision. Due to the concentration of dispatching and administrative personnel at Denison in 1959 and the later abolishment of passenger service, the Muskogee station was deemed a tax liability and was wiped from the books through demolition in the mid-1960's. This photograph was snapped on the morning of October 19, 1963. *(Earl Holloway)*

*(Above)* Combination caboose #342 was found on the storage tracks of Dallas Yard during August 1965, waiting for final disposition. This interesting car was in surprisingly good condition and still wore its original "Sloan Yellow" paint scheme. Ten cars, numbered 341-350, were built in the MKT's Denison car shops in 1942 for use in mixed branch line service. No. 342 provided seating for a maximum of 18 passengers and had been used on the local between Dallas and Denton, Texas in the early 1960's. Even after June 30, 1965, rail aficionados could still obtain caboose or locomotive rides by simply requesting a trip pass from Katy President John Barriger, who was a railfan himself and proud of it. *(John B. Charles)*

*(Above)* The Katy depot at Waco, Texas became expendable after passenger service south of Dallas was abolished on July 26, 1964. The MKT could not justify the expense of maintaining this large station, which resulted in its demolition during 1967. *(J.O.B. Johnson)*

*(Right)* This Sloan-era station sign at Highland Park, Texas was illuminated with neon lights at nighttime and had been on display since the mid-1930's. Shortly after the abandonment of passenger service in 1965, this unique suburban facility was razed. Destruction of such historic stations was later mourned by most of the communities served by the MKT. The photo dates from March 14, 1965. *(William J. Neill)*

*(Above)*  Straight from the Parsons, Kansas wash racks was modified Alco FA-1 #84C, idling between assignments in Dallas Yard on July 22, 1965.  Re-engined in 1959 by EMD with a 16-cylinder 567C power plant, this unit wears the livery of the Deramus-Williams regimes.  An obvious addition on top of #84C's revised main-roof hatch is a new set of spark arresters, installed on most Katy engines in 1965 and one of the first of many changes made during Mr. Barriger's presidency.
*(John B. Charles)*

*(Left)*  The sale of Katy's nine EMD E-8s to Precision Engineering was arranged as soon as passenger service ceased on July 1, 1965. Fourteen unsightly Alco PA hulks were finally laid to rest through sales to salvage dealers Commercial Metals and Hyman Michaels during the last quarter of 1965. Commercial Metals had earlier scrapped the two E-7s, #101A and #101C, in 1964.  By December 31, 1965 the Katy power fleet was reduced to 180 units.

A happier end came for ex-Katy E-8A #54A, photographed at Atlanta, Georgia on July 9, 1966 wearing the Atlantic Coast Line's black and yellow livery, as well as a new number, 553.  All but one of the ex-Katy E-8s were sold by Precision Engineering to the ACL.  Four of these units (ex-Katy #52A, 52C, 53A and 53C) eventually were used in AMTRAK service. *(William J. Neill)*

(Above) In January 1966, this northbound train prepares to get underway at Bellmead Yard, 2.5 miles north of Waco, Texas, with modified FA-1 #83C on the point. Booster power was provided by an F-9 B unit and another FA. On April 5, 1965, President Barriger had authorized a second St. Louis train, restoration of daily (except Sunday) branch line service, the return of local trains on the mainline and additional switchers at major terminals. This surge in operations necessitated the extended use of every unit of power available to the Katy, which made for some unorthodox power lash-ups. Katy spotters of the 1960's never knew what would be seen rolling down the line next. *(Dr. Tom Hughes)*

(Below) Moving at 40 miles per hour, modified FA-1 #82A is blaring its horns at a grade crossing at Itasca, Texas, as it wheels the tonnage of train No. 4 northward in August 1966. No. 4 departed Houston the previous evening and was scheduled to arrive in Knasas City at 9:00 AM the following day, providing dependable second morning service. One year earlier, on August 9, 1965, this and two other daily Houston-to-Kansas City trains had been established by President Barriger. *(John B. Charles)*

*(Left)* On May 3, 1966, F-3 #64C is the lead unit of train No. 63, "in the hole" at Pottsboro, Texas, only 8.7 miles southwest of Denison on the Katy's Ft. Worth Subdivision. No. 63 is waiting for a northbound Missouri Pacific train that has already passed the joint station at Whitesboro, 16 miles to the south. The MKT's old Victorian-era frame depot at Pottsboro had been built in about 1880 and was still in use, providing Monday through Friday telegraph service for only a few more months prior to its permanent closing. A section of double track mainline was in service at Pottsboro, as well as a connecting spur track that served nearby Perrin Air Force Base.

After the meet, No. 63 will proceed south to Whitesboro, then west on the 106 mile Henrietta Subdivision to Wichita Falls, Texas. This train and eastbound No. 64 were every-other-day locals to and from Wichita Falls. *(William J. Neill)*

(Above)  Alco cab unit #85A and modified Baldwin AS-16 #124 were at Waxahatchie, Texas in August 1966 with a northbound train.  The familiar smoke and clattering rumble of Katy's two remaining Alco-engined FA-1s, #85A and #85C, would be seen and heard no more after their trade-in to EMD the following year.

Although poor track conditions at Waxahatchie did not permit *fast* freight service, John Barriger made certain the new schedules were at least dependable. (*John B. Charles*)

(*Opposite, below*)  At the Smithville, Texas enginehouse in February 1966 was #144, one of nine Alco RS-3 road-switchers that were never modified. Other than a shiny new paint job and newly applied adhesive-backed Katy emblems, #144 is identical to its as-delivered appearance in 1950. This fact is indicative of the overall success of Alco's general purpose design on the Katy; so, "If it works, don't fix it." No. 144 was traded in to EMD in 1967, when new GP-40's were purchased. (*Dr.Tom Hughes*)

(*Above*)  The Waxahachie, Texas passenger station was an important point on the MKT's Hillsboro Subdivision.  Built in 1908 of brick with a red tile roof, this was a joint agency with the Ft. Worth & Denver in the mid-1960's, with gross earnings for 1966 totalling $1,214,849.  The rail in the photograph at the top of this page was 115 lb. laid in 1947-48, and is in sharp contrast to the track conditions in this photo, taken Feb. 14, 1981.  In 1977 several sections of heavy welded rail were laid on the line between Dallas and Waxahachie, in addition to surfacing improvements.  (*Earl Holloway*)

(Above)  In 1965 twenty-five urgently needed new cabooses were ordered from International Car Company, as a result of the increased number of trains.  Caboose #100 of the new 100-124 series was photographed at Dallas Yard in August 1966.  With this series, the Katy began the custom of stenciling "RADIO EQUIPPED" with thunderbolt highlights on the side panels of the wide-vision cupolas.

In addition to new equipment, Mr. Barriger authorized a program to rehabilitate twenty-seven existing way cars at the Denison car shops beginning in June 1965 when the shops were reactivated.  Car repair facilities at Denison's Ray Yard and Parsons, Kansas were also reopened and together restored 1,181 freight cars to active service during the last half of 1965.  *(John B. Charles)*

*(Above)*  Southbound train No. 1 is underway again at Dallas on a clear August morning in 1966.  This train had been inaugurated on July 1, 1965 (the day after the discontinuance of passenger service) between Kansas City and Dallas;  it made connections at Kansas City with overnight trains from Chicago and also expedited the arrival of cars from St. Louis.  On August 9, 1965, No. 1's route had been extended from Dallas to Houston.  The power lineup this day was an interesting mixture of original and rebuilt road units, with EMD F-3 #65A in the lead followed by two morphidite AS-16s and a modified FA unit.  Although this crazy quilt of power appears quite diverse, train No. 1 was in reality powered by a solid formation of EMD prime movers.  *(John B. Charles)*

*(Opposite page, top)*  Wearing the livery of the new Katy president, switcher #28, a modified Baldwin DS44-1000, shuffles two brand new cabooses around at the south end of Dallas Yard on a typically warm August afternoon in 1966.  At the extreme right, Katy business cars #400 and 401 were on their storage tracks, indicating President Barriger was probably in town.  *(John B. Charles)*

*(Opposite page, bottom)*  As with the Deramus and Williams administrations, President Barriger acquired new equipment through long-term lease rather than installment purchase.  In 1966 four hundred thirty-seven old box cars were sold, modernized and leased back to the Katy.  The renewed cars arrived during the last quarter of 1966 and early 1967.  Wearing the new Barriger paint scheme, a group of rebuilt 40'6" box cars, including #6696, has just been returned to the Katy's Baden Yard at St. Louis, Missouri in 1967.  A total of 2,595 new and 702 rebuilt freight cars were leased and placed in service during 1967, bringing Katy's freight car ownership up to 11,144 cars, with the bad order ratio lowered to 4.9% of the fleet.
*(Fred Lyon, dec., University of Missouri-Columbia/Western Manuscripts Collection)*

*(Right)* Dispatcher G.E. Canaday handles all movements on the Southern Division from the Denison, Texas office on the second floor of the old passenger station on May 19, 1968. Notice the telegraph key and sounder that were still being used for communications with depots in western Oklahoma. *(John B. Charles)*

Part of the charm of the Katy Railroad was its steadfast reliance on classic railroad operating methods. Katy trains of 1988 were operated almost exactly as they had been in 1928 through the use of published timetables, train orders and the standard book of rules. At the heart of Katy operations was its corps of veteran dispatchers, who were the masters of everything that transpired on the rails of their respective territories. Only the Chief Dispatcher and system level officials had more authority than a Katy train dispatcher. The importance of these dispatchers stemmed from the fact that the MKT was basically a single-track railroad, with limited block signal protection. The dispatcher had the lives of every man on the line in his hands at all times. Into the late 1980's, north and south end dispatchers still communicated orders to distant operators who continued to copy two complete sets (forward and rear) for pick-up by designated trains. This process was only slightly different than methods used sixty years earlier. To its last day, Katy management believed train orders were an essential safety double-check for its radio-dispatched orders, especially in non-CTC single-track territory.

*(Opposite, above)* New yard caboose #71 was in service at Ray Yard, Denison, Texas, with modified RS-3 #146 in April 1967. This and another homemade caboose, #70, were built on old underframes during 1966-67 and equipped with footboards, but no radio.

During this period, eight engine shifts were being worked at Ray Yard, which made this the third busiest terminal on the system behind the yards at Dallas and Houston, Texas. Earlier, between 1957 and 1960, Ray had been rebuilt into a modern saucer-type classification yard by the Deramus management team. Because of the lack of funds, a planned multi-purpose freight and passenger station was never constructed at this location. *(John B. Charles)*

*(Opposite page, below)* The old yard office at Ray Yard had been freshly spray painted in this view from September 7, 1968. A colorful enameled Sloan-era engine herald was proudly displayed from the second story. Katy operators stationed in this office remotely controlled the approach signals and interlocker at the Red River Bridge, five miles north of Ray. The Missouri Pacific and Frisco roads shared the usage of the bridge through trackage rights agreements with the MKT at that time.

Also visible to the right is ex-troop sleeper #102413 that was used as a kitchen-diner by maintenance-of-way and wrecker outfit gangs. *(Earl Holloway)*

*(Above)* With the mainline engulfed in grass, this northbound train is underway again after handling local work at Granger, Texas on a June afternoon in 1966. President Barriger was forced to prolong the Deramus-Williams program of deferred track maintenance because of multi-million dollar deficits in 1965 and 1966; however, eleven miles of automatic block signals were placed in service in 1966 between Granger and Taylor, Texas. Caboose #47, built in 1930, had been recently outshopped in the bright Barriger paint scheme and brings up the rear. *(Dr. Tom Hughes)*

(Above)   The depot at Granger, Texas was still wearing the two-toned green paint scheme of the 1920's when photographed on February 8, 1968. Since 1905, Granger had been the junction point of the San Antonio and Houston Subdivisions, but thru trains passed on by starting in January 1965 when the Katy begain using 35 miles of trackage rights on the Missouri Pacific between Taylor and Austin, Texas. The Missouri Pacific was accorded reciprocal privileges on MKT trackage from Ft. Worth to Waco, Texas (85 miles). This arrangement provided a shorter route to San Antonio and triggered Katy's abandonment of 32 miles of its own line into Austin in 1976. The remaining 15 mile branch line between Granger and Georgetown became very valuable to the Katy because of the extraordinary growth of a tiny new shortline named the Georgetown Railroad. By 1970 the GRR was delivering 100-car unit rock trains to the Katy at Georgetown from its parent Texas Crushed Stone Co. The majority of these trains were conveyed to a TCS facility adjacent to Katy's Eureka Yard at Houston, then experiencing an unparalleled building boom.

(Left)   Although deferred maintenance was apparent on many parts of the Katy in 1966, John Barriger moved forward with a program to upgrade track conditions on the Oklahoma mainline and in north Texas. In August 1966, pile driver #X-1030 was in action rebuilding a trestle near Royse City, Texas, thirty-six miles northeast of Dallas Yard. The self-propelled diesel pile driver was built by American Hoist & Derrick Co. of St. Paul, Minnesota and had been acquired in 1957 by President Deramus. While this work progressed, 16.6 miles of 115 lb. continuous welded rail was being laid on the Ft. Worth Subdivision, between Denison and Sadler, Texas, and near Muskogee, Oklahoma. This two-year project involved relaying 34 miles of rail and was a milestone in M-K-T annals, being the first welded rail laid. (Both-John B. Charles)

(Above) The balmy temperatures of this beautiful January day in 1967 are being enjoyed by the crew of modified Baldwin switcher #27. These men have just returned to Dallas Yard from their morning's work on nearby industry tracks with a cut of cars and are nearing the end of their 6:30 AM-to-2:30 PM shift. Gross station earnings rose to $18.9 million in 1967, making Dallas, by far, the Katy's most valuable agency; a total of fifteen assigned engine shifts were being worked from this yard. EMD F-7A #72A was also in the yard this day, resplendent in the new Barriger paint scheme. With the elimination of the fireman position, the Katy equipped fifty-six road units with automatic alertness controls in 1967. Another more noticeable alteration made to #72A and thirty-five other cab units, between 1966 and 1968, was the addition of multiple-unit nose receptacles, which permitted their use as booster power. (John B. Charles)

(Below) On September 7, 1968, this northbound train is underway at Denison's Ray Yard behind EMD GP-7 #100 and an unknown F-3A unit. In the distance to the left is the Ray roundhouse and power station that were being partially demolished at that time. To the right is a massive new Pillsbury foods plant, served exclusively by the MKT. (Earl Holloway)

John Barriger stepped up public relations activities in 1967 through the sponsorship of several high profile inspection trips across the system in April and September. An additional special train was operated in June from Wichita Falls to join in the 75th anniversary celebration of the historic oil boomtown of Burkburnett, Texas. Other public relations efforts involved the hiring of famed railroad artist Howard Fogg to paint a series of watercolors depicting the Katy from its early days to the present. A first-rate advertising program was formulated that featured the new "Miss Katy" in printed ads. The daily press was kept informed of important Katy projects and responded with a flood of favorable attention. More good publicity came from feature articles appearing in national publications such as *Trains* magazine, written in most cases by David P. Morgan, a longtime personal friend of Mr. Barriger. The following views are of one of the special inspection trains that became a Barriger trademark in the late 1960's.

*(Above)* Passing between the stone overpass abutments of a long abandoned Rock Island branch line, a brace of gleaming FP-7s powers this Katy inspection train south through the scenic foothills of the Kiamichi Mountains near Kiowa, Oklahoma in April 1967. Although #81C and its mate still possessed their steam boilers, power car #100187 was providing electricity and heat to the four passenger cars of the train. All Katy passenger locomotives had been sold or the boilers removed from most of the remaining dual-service units by this date, which necessitated the use of #100187, a former baggage car that had been converted to a generator car for the wrecker outfit train. Water for the power car's two steam boilers and the passenger equipment was provided by modified tank car #100188. In addition to the two MKT business cars #400 and 401, a Pullman sleeper and a Missouri Pacific lounge car have been leased for the three day trip.
*(John B. Charles)*

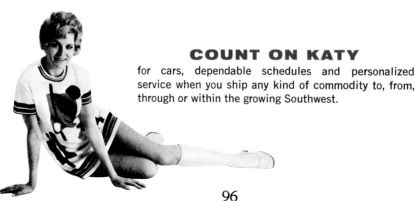

**COUNT ON KATY**
for cars, dependable schedules and personalized service when you ship any kind of commodity to, from, through or within the growing Southwest.

*(Below)* The sun is setting on the second day of the trip as the inspection extra stops at the Denison, Texas passenger station for the night. Semiannual trips were arranged to provide the managers of the various Katy sales offices a firsthand view of the railroad's facilities and typically included a major sales meeting at some point along the route. Guests had opportunities for one-on-one discussions with Mr. Barriger and his headquarters staff, plus a close-up look at the progress being made in rebuilding the MKT. *(John B. Charles)*

*(Above)* Morning of the third day found the inspection train moving southbound at 60 mph near Royse City, Texas on the Dallas Subdivision. In spite of the fact Mr. Barriger could not afford to upgrade the 90 lb. rail of this 105 mile subdivision, eighty-six miles of right-of-way were surfaced, lined and dressed during 1966 and 1967. *(John B. Charles)*

John Barriger had warned the principal stockholders in 1965 that he would be an expensive luxury; in fact, he later concluded at least $100 million would be needed to rebuild the Katy. Deficits in 1965 and 1966 were outpaced in 1967 by a staggering loss of $10.5 million, although Mr. Barriger was quick to point out that Katy's car and locomotive replacement program was probably the largest ever undertaken by any railroad, in relation to its size. To cut expenses and improve profitability, the Katy acquired I.C.C. approval in 1967 to abandon 220 miles of the Rotan Subdivision betweem Waco and Stamford, Texas. The 43-mile Stamford-to-Rotan branch was retained and an outlet from Stamford to the MKT at Wichita Falls was provided through 113 miles of trackage rights over the Ft. Worth & Denver. The abandoned line was the major part of the former Texas Central Railroad, acquired by the Katy in 1910.

*(Left)* The old Texas Central-built depot at Hamlin, Texas was located 246 miles west of the Katy mainline at Waco and only 22 miles east of the end-of-track at Rotan. Communication between the Denison dispatcher and the Hamlin operator was strictly by telegraph when this photo was taken on April 4, 1965. As if forgotten by time, the depot still wore the peeling yellow paint and enameled herald of the Matthew Sloan administration. Track conditions on the Stamford-to-Rotan line were possibly the worst on the MKT, with the pictured rail being 56 lb. resting on bare west Texas prairie. Two large gypsum plants, one at Hamlin and the other at Rotan, accounted for combined station earnings for both agencies of over $1.1 million in 1967. This 43 mile orphan branch was eventually sold to the Ft. Worth & Denver in 1973. *(John B. Charles)*

*(Right)* On December 12, 1967, an elderly F-9 B unit is sandwiched between two new EMD GP-40s, led by #176, as this northbound train crosses a timber trestle north of Smithville, Texas on the Katy's Texas Subdivision. A dozen new 3,000 HP GP-40s (#182-193) arrived in 1967 to join the first group of twelve that were purchased in 1966 (#170-181). By the close of 1967 the MKT owned 183 well-maintained engines, with the locomotive bad order ratio reduced to a sensational 3.3%. *(John B. Charles)*

*(Opposite page, below)* Photographer John Charles climbed on the roof of a box car to get this excellent view of boiler-equipped GP-7 #121 working in the yard at DeLeon, Texas for the last time on November 28, 1967. This was the cleanup train that made the last trip on the Rotan Subdivision, formerly the Texas Central Railroad, prior to its abandonment. No. 121 and F-3 #64A pulled thirty-eight loaded cars and six empties off the branch line nicknamed the T.C. or "Tin Can," arriving at Bellmead Yard at 4:10 the following morning. Interestingly, a Texas Central shortline lives on today because of the purchase of 25 miles of the old line between Dublin and Gorman, Texas by a group of local businessmen for $70 thousand in 1967. The remaining nearly 200 miles of line was sold to salvage contractors for $750,000, which was immediately plowed back into the Barriger improvement program.

*(Below)* Back on the mainline, the engineer of Houston-bound No. 1 gives a friendly wave as his train stirs up the dust of the grade crossing near the Katy depot at Taylor, Texas on May 15, 1968. The lead unit is new EMD GP-40 #186, followed by aging F-7 #77C and another new "Geep." South of Taylor, No. 1's route to Houston was entirely on Katy rails, whereas trains bound for San Antonio crossed over to the tracks of the Missouri Pacific at the switch located just north of the pictured block signal. *(John B. Charles)*

(*Left*) GP-40s #196 and #171 are assisted by an unknown F-3 cab unit in powering this northbound train at Granger, Texas in January 1970. Although a lower semaphore blade is missing, this train has a clear board and green lights to proceed into the 62 mile section of automatic block signal territory between Granger and Bellmead Yard. The dramatic drop-off of business in the late 1950's caused the Deramus administration to dismantle 176 miles of block signals between Granger and Houston in 1959. In fact, Mr. Deramus was said to have considered abandoning the entire Houston Subdivision prior to his departure in 1961. President Barriger quickly reversed this policy, but could only afford the cost of restoring eleven miles of block signals between Granger and the Missouri Pacific connection at Taylor, Texas. Trains to and from Houston operated entirely by train orders and were otherwise "blind," until the Houston Subdivision was finally rebuilt in the mid-1970's. (*John B. Charles*)

(*Left*) Southbound train No. 3 is crossing the tracks of the Frisco Railroad on the diamond adjacent to the joint station at Durant, Oklahoma on the morning of June 20, 1970. No. 3 was a Kansas City-to-Houston train that left K.C. on the evening of the 19th, with arrival time at Houston's Eureka Yard set for 5:00 AM the morning of the 21st. Three new GP-40s are in the power lineup, along with a GP-7 and one of the few surviving F-7 units, #77A. By the close of 1970, only twelve cab units, nicknamed "Roundnosers," remained on the Katy roster; these included three F-3As, five F-7As and four FP-7s. The balance had been sold to Precision Engineering or traded in to EMD in exchange for new power. (*Earl Holloway*)

*(Above)*  A lineup of four new 3,000 HP GP-40s, led by #198 rolls through the bustling college town of Denton, Texas on August 15, 1970.  As indicated by the emblems on the freight house to the right, Denton was a combined agency on joint trackage with the Missouri Pacific-controlled Texas & Pacific Railroad.  This 72 mile section was between Whitesboro and Ft. Worth, Texas on the Katy's Ft. Worth Subdivision.  Starting in the 1880's, the two roads agreed to share the income and expenses of this line on an equal basis and began the practice of alternating the operation of local train service on the joint track every three months.  The agent of the joint station had a difficult and thankless job, since he was required to be completely impartial in handling business and accounting matters between these two railroads that were, as a rule, aggressive competitors.  *(Earl Holloway)*

*(Right)*    President Barriger's five year campaign (1965-1970) to make the MKT the "best dressed" and most well-equipped railroad for its size in the Southwest was calculated to increase investor confidence and attract a suitable merger partner; however, Katy was to wait another eighteen years for her brokered marriage to the Union Pacific.

Included in the group of seventy-one new locomotives acquired between 1966 and 1969 were six SW-1500 switch engines, #50-55.  Working in Dallas Yard on August 15, 1970 was #52, built by EMD in 1968.  With the arrival of the new 1,500 HP switchers, the gradual retirement of twelve unmodified Baldwin S-12 units began.  By mid-1971 eight Baldwins had been wiped from the roster through trade-in to EMD or sold as scrap, while the remaining four units (#40, 41, 45 and 47) went to work in south Texas on the Georgetown Railroad. *(Earl Holloway)*

(Above) The well-powered second section of northbound train No. 2 roars off the Katy's Red River Bridge into the state of Oklahoma on June 21, 1970. An indication of the Katy's bleak business picture is illustrated by the fact that at no time during the years 1965 - 1967 was it necessary to operate *any* scheduled train with a second section. However, starting in 1968 second sections of southbound No. 3 became a relatively frequent occurrence at Kansas City. By 1970 additional sections were being seen often across the system, as traffic levels began a gradual and sustained increase. *(Earl Holloway)*

*(Opposite page, top)* The northbound daily local, No. 54, is rolling into Denison, Texas from its morning run on the Dallas Subdivision behind two "Barriger Red" GP-40s, with #223 on the point. The date: June 20, 1970. Although the MKT was providing excellent service to a growing number of shippers, 1970 was the seventh consecutive year of deficit net income, with a loss of $3.5 million that year.
*(Earl Holloway)*

*(Opposite page, bottom)* The final group of new locomotives acquired during the Barriger improvement program were four 2,200 HP EMD GP-38s numbered 300-303, delivered to the Katy in December 1969. At Dallas Yard on April 12, 1970 were #300 and 301 of the new series awaiting their next road assignment. President Barriger was proud of the fact that the total number of locmotives had been reduced from 208 units on December 1, 1964, to 181 in 1970. The 71 new EMD road and switch engines represented fifty-seven per cent of Katy's power fleet and cost $14.5 million, a bargan price by the later inflated standards of the 1970's and 80's.
*(Earl Holloway)*

(Above) At seventy, John Barriger had been allowed a five year extension of the Katy's normal policy of retirement at age 65; his last day as president finally came on July 14, 1970. When not on the road preaching Katy's gospel to shippers or lending institutions, Mr. Barriger had lived aboard Business Car #400 at Dallas, Texas. Nos. 400 & 401 and power car #100187 were provided for his convenience on a section of rented track at Dallas Union Terminal, as seen here in August 1970. No. 400 had been construced in the Katy's Sedalia car shops in 1929 for M.H. Cahill, Chairman of the Board and later President of the MKT, whom Barriger had personally known in his earlier days as a transportation stock analyst. Mr. Barriger enjoyed carrying on the traditions of fine dining and Katy hospitality by inviting guests to breakfast with him each morning aboard #400. Not a drinking man himself, Barriger found breakfast an ideal way to conduct business without the embarrassment of refusing alcohol at lunch or dinner meetings. In addition, as he once quipped, "I've never had to worry about adjourning a breakfast meeting. Also, breakfast is the least expensive meal of the day." *(John B. Charles)*

(Above) Baldwin S-12 switcher #47 handles a train of salvageable 85 lb. rail and ties on October 13, 1970 at Gainesville, Texas, during the dismantling of the Henrietta Subdivision. Prior to his July 1970 departure, President Barriger had received I.C.C. approval to abandon 99 miles of this subdivision between Whitesboro and Wichita Falls, Texas. Starting in 1968, trackage rights on the Ft. Worth & Denver (Burlington Route) were used from Ft. Worth to Wichita Falls to maintain service to that vicinity and provide an outlet for the MKT's isolated Western Subdivision. *(Earl Holloway)*

(Below) Great Britain's famous FLYING SCOTSMAN steam locomotive and its accompanying set of exhibition coaches were run on the MKT between Temple, Texas and Kansas City, Missouri during June of 1970. The train was on a two year tour of the U.S. and Canada and had spent the winter of 1969-1970 in the Santa Fe's shops at Slaton, Texas. Seen here at Waco, Texas, on June 17, 1970, is the northbound FLYING SCOTSMAN, receiving some help from switch engine #28, a modified Baldwin DS44-1000 that had been assigned to pilot the train to nearby Bellmead Yard for servicing. *(Emery J. Gulash)*

*(Above)* A southbound train is ready to depart Forgan, Oklahoma on September 20, 1972 behind GP-7 #112. Trains operating on this most distant Katy subdivision took two days to travel the 303 mile route between Forgan and North Yard at Wichita Falls, Texas. The deteriorated condition of the Western Subdivision's 60 and 65 lb. rail and unballasted roadbed restricted speed limits to a maximum of 10 mph. During 1972 limited service was still provided on the 105 mile subsidiary Beaver, Meade & Englewood, nicknamed "The Beaver Road," which began at Forgan and extended into the Oklahoma panhandle to the town of Keyes where an interchange track was maintained with the Santa Fe. As early as 1964 the MKT had considered the abandonment of a major portion of the Western Subdivision; however, annual wheat harvests continued to be a valuable part of the Katy's net income until final abandonment of all lines north of Altus, Oklahoma came in 1973. The frame depot and small yard at Forgan had been constructed when the line was built in 1912 by the Wichita Falls & Northwestern Railway Co. *(Earl Holloway)*

*(Right)* In 1911 the M.K.&T. acquired control of the Wichita Falls & Northwestern Railway from the original operators, J.A. Kemp and Frank Kell of Wichita Falls. The WF&NW included the mainline from Wichita Falls to Forgan, as well as a 56 mile branch line between Altus, Oklahoma and Wellington, Texas.

As pictured on September 19, 1972, the depot at Woodward, Oklahoma was an excellent example of WF&NW station architecture. In addition to local business, Woodward was an interchange point between the Katy and the Santa Fe. After abandonment by the MKT in 1973, a new shortline named the Northwestern Oklahoma Railroad began operations at Woodward to continue service to local customers through the Santa Fe connection. Apart from track segments at Woodward and another shortline spinoff at Altus, the remaining 330 mile line between Altus and Keyes was scrapped in 1973. *(Earl Holloway)*

107

(Above) Idling on the service tracks of the Denison enginehouse on June 10, 1972 is EMD GP-7 #121. The Katy acquired thirty-three GP-7s between 1950 and 1952, numbering them #1501-1529 and #1761-1764. The four latter engines were delivered with steam boilers and electrical generators for use as back-up passenger power; they were outwardly distinguished from freight-only GP-7s by the placement of the air reservoir tanks on top of their long hoods. In 1960, the GP-7s were renumbered #91-123, with the passenger units designated #120-123. After passenger service ended in 1965, several modifications were made to the ex-passenger Geeps. As illustrated by this photo, the boiler and upper headlights have been removed from #121, although a distinctive set of four blended air horns and the high-mounted air tanks remain in place. (Earl Holloway)

(Left) This view of EMD GP-38 #300 at Houston's Eureka Yard in December 1971 is a study of utilitarian automation in repose. No new power was acquired by President Whitman during his first few years, as he concentrated on improving the Katy's physical plant. In Mr. Whitman's words, "There's no use buying locomotives capable of traveling 90 miles per hour and putting them on tracks limited to 10 miles per hour." During 1971 seventy-two miles of track was rehabilitated. Also, an automobile unloading facility was constructed in Tulsa, Oklahoma and a new combination pile driver-derrick-ditcher was purchased for the maintenance-of-way program. (John B. Charles)

(Above)  Twin GP-40s are cracking the whip, as a southbound train rolls by the old yard office at Parsons, Kansas on June 9, 1973.  This train will traverse the 117 mile Cherokee Subdivision from Parsons to the crew change point at Muskogee, Oklahoma, on its route to Texas destinations.  By 1973, recovery on the Katy was well underway with gross income increasing to over $90 million, the highest earnings in the road's history.  Paradoxically, President Whitman experienced his first Missouri River flood in 1973;  large portions of the 189 mile St. Louis Subdivision were severely damaged.  Although 1973 earnings were outstanding, the MKT had a surprisingly low ratio of maintenance-of-way expenses to total operating revenues of 12.94%.  This figure indicates the flood repairs caused track work on most other sections of the railroad to be deferred.  (Earl Holloway)

(Below)  A program to lower the short hoods of all Katy GP-7s got underway in February 1971 when #123 was revised at the Parsons locomotive shops.  In addition to a lowered nose, #123 was also the first unit to wear a new yellow and green paint scheme.  Two more GP-7s were revised in December 1971, #110 and #116;  however, these units returned to duty wearing their Barriger-era paint schemes and were the only modified units that were painted red for a brief time.  Consequently, this glimpse of red chop-nosed #116 in switching service at St. Louis, Missouri on May 19, 1973, is quite rare.  (Mel Nierdieck)

(Above) Although the new green and yellow paint scheme looked quite striking on FP-7 #81A, photographed at Denison's Ray Yard on June 23, 1974, this unit was sold to Percision Engineering only three months later. The stub-nosed newcomer adjacent to #81A was General Electric U23B #351, purchased with sister units #350 and 352 in May 1973. These handsome units were the first non-EMD power acquired by the Katy in twenty years and unfortunately proved to be the last. Almost immediately, the GEs required additional amounts of downtime for servicing and repairs because of a myriad of major and minor problems. Unfamiliarity with General Electric's maintenance system and the lack of an adequate GE parts inventory appear to have been the chief causes of the early failure of these engines.

(Below) Same date. U23B #351 and GP-40 #230 prepare to get underway with a northbound train at Denison. As the three 2250 horsepower GEs encountered an increasing amount of mechanical problems, their runs were scheduled to keep them in proximity to the Parsons, Kansas locomotive shops. Eventually, their last assignments were in branch line service between Parsons and Chanute, Kansas and in the Parsons yards, prior to their trade-in to EMD in January 1984. (Both- Earl Holloway)

In a continuing effort to operate more profitably, the Whitman administration sought and received permission from the Interstate Commerce Commission in 1977 to abandon 145 miles of the Katy's Oklahoma Subdivision between Bartlesville and Oklahoma City. At the height of Oklahoma's historic oil boom in 1915, the Katy had run twelve to fifteen trains daily, north and southbound, from its division point at Osage, Oklahoma. After abandonment, Katy service to Oklahoma City continued through a trackage rights agreement with the Rock Island Lines for operation between McAlester, on the MKT mainline, and Oklahoma City. This 117 mile section was eventually purchased by the Katy from the receiver of the bankrupt Rock Island in 1984.

*(Above)* A southbound local, powered by two F-7s and a GP-7, has stopped at the joint AT&SF-MKT station at Bartlesville, Oklahoma on August 23, 1975. Bartlesville was a significant point on the Katy's 208 mile Oklahoma Subdivision, from Parsons, Kansas to Oklahoma City, Oklahoma. Several of the larger buildings in the background housed the headquarters of the Phillips Petroleum Company, a major shipper on the Katy for many years. Operators in this handsome station controlled the interlocking plant at D.Y. Junction (Dewey, Oklahoma), 3.2 miles north of the depot, where Katy trains utilized trackage rights to operate on a 4.5 mile section of the Santa Fe. After receiving clearance from the Bartlesville operator, this train will move south to B.E. Junction, where it will return to Katy trackage. In addition to through service, the MKT and Santa Fe rotated the assignment of a switch engine and crew at Bartlesville to serve local industries and handle yard work. *(Earl Holloway)*

*(Right)* Exercising newly acquired trackage rights on 117 miles of the Rock Island's "Sunbelt Route" between McAlester and Oklahoma City, this eastbound train is passing the picturesque mission style depot at Seminole, Oklahoma with an eastbound train on September 30, 1977. Power was supplied by two veteran cab units: FP-7 #78C and F-7 #72C. These two anomalies were in regularly assigned turnaround service on the Oklahoma City line during 1977 and 1978, attracting national coverage in *Trains* and *Railfan* magazines. After later systemwide service, primarily as booster power, #72C and #78C were dismantled at Parsons in 1980. *(Earl Holloway)*

*(Above)* Inspection car #1045 is riding the rear of a southbound train as it arrives at Denison's Ray Yard on the afternoon of February 7, 1976. Visible in the observation compartment is Vice President of Operations Harold L. Gastler, who frequently used #1045 for the close examination of track conditions systemwide. Despite its homemade appearance, #1045 was an excellent example of Katy ingenuity. Deprived of the comforts of business cars #400 and 401 in 1971 because of their sale to the Georgetown Railroad, then Vice President of Operations Billy R. Bishop developed a plan for the construction of a specialized inspection car. Constructed in the Denison car shops in 1973, #1045 was unlike anything used previously on the Katy, or any other U.S. railroad for that matter. Although equipped with state-of-the-art conveniences such as air conditioning, radio telephone and a large observation compartment with comfortable seating, #1045 could not entirely overcome its box car origins. In spite of the use of roller-bearing leaf-spring type caboose trucks, the inspection car was said to have ridden like a box car because of its inherent top-heavy design and relative light overall weight. In 1989, after the formal merger of the MKT and Union Pacific, #1045 was given to the city of Denison; however, after months of inactivity on the part of city officials as to where to place the car for display, it was quietly moved out of Ray Yard by the Union Pacific and sold to an interested party. *(Earl Holloway)*

*(Left)* The Katy's pride in its self reliance and recent success was evident across the system in the mid-1970s, as demonstrated by this company fuel tank truck, photographed at Denison on April 13, 1974. The truck had been freshly painted "Whitman Green," with a stenciled yellow Katy emblem on its side, while its green and yellow-striped front bumper echoed the bright new locomotive paint schemes. Katy employees were proud of the fact that annual gross revenues were the highest in the MKT's history, even outpacing the enormous World War II amounts earned by their fathers and grandfathers. Revenues were rising at the rate of about 15% each year, which was among the highest gain ratios in the industry among major roads. *(Earl Holloway)*

*(Above)* The bicentennial year of 1976 was made memorable on the Katy and most U.S. railroads by painting one or more pieces of rolling stock in patriotic colors for the year-long celebration. It was appropriate that GP-40 #200, built by EMD in 1968, was selected by the mechanical department to be honored as the MKT's standard bearer. The beautiful new paint job appears to be very fresh in this view taken at Dallas Yard during October 1975 and even included white-trimmed wheels, reminiscent of highlighted drivers, *à la* Katy steam power. To the disappointment of rail buffs and photographers, #200 was repainted in the standard livery by the end of 1977. As late as 1993, this locomotive was still in service on the Union Pacific and was reportedly one of the last ex-Katy units remaining in green and yellow paint. *(Mike Bledsoe)*

*(Above)* Bicentennial caboose #76 is rolling past Tower 55 at Ft. Worth, Texas with a southbound train on a splendid November afternoon in 1976. Unlike GP-40 #200, the Katy's mechanical department seems to have had no logical reason for selecting caboose #130 to be repainted as bicentennial caboose #76; this car was apparently at the Denison shops for routine maintenance at just the right time. Built by the Darby Corporation of Kansas City, Kansas in 1968, #130 and nine identical units, numbered 125-134, were very similar to the #100-124 series constructed two years earlier by International Car Company. In 1990, after caboose #130 had been given to the city of Windsor, Missouri for static display by the Union Pacific, its bicentennial paint job was discovered under a layer of green and yellow paint by volunteers who were sandblasting the car. The decision was made to carefully restore the caboose to its patriotic 1976 colors. No. 76 is now completely restored and has become the prized centerpiece of this community, located on the Katy's former Sedalia Subdivision. *(Mike Bledsoe)*

*(Above)* On June 18, 1977, this southbound grain extra was restricted to a 20 mph speed limit as it rolled through the Waco, Texas commercial district on its route to the Gulf of Mexico and the export grain centers of Houston and Galveston. Four units, led by GP-40 #180, were powering this train over Waco Creek with #200, the bicentennial engine, being the last unit in the power lineup. One mile south of this bridge, the hogger was allowed to kick the speed up to 40 mph for the charge up Waco Hill, which rises abruptly out of the Brazos River bottoms. This was the first of several notable grades encountered through the rolling countryside south of Waco on the Katy's 127 mile Texas Subdivision, between the division points of Bellmead and Smithville, Texas. The year 1977 saw a continuation of record breaking achievements on the Katy with total operating revenues climbing to $117,186,000, an increase of 16% over 1976 earnings. An improved economic atmosphere during 1977 resulted in a remarkable increase of 56% in motor vehicle carloadings alone. *(Earl Holloway)*

*(Left)* In 1977, President R.N. Whitman expressed his support for the formation of a separate Katy Railroad Historical Society by allowing a tour for the group at its first meeting at Parsons, Kansas on October 1, 1977. Forty-three charter members attended that first gathering. The cavernous main bay of the Parsons locomotive shops was visited during the tour, where General Electric U23B #350 was found undergoing repairs. Twenty-two locomotives received remanufactured main generators at the Parsons shops during 1977. *(Earl Holloway)*

116

*(Right)* GP-38 #303 and northbound train No. 106 are working at Katy, Texas on December 20, 1977. The town of Katy is 24 miles northwest of Houston's Eureka Yard on the MKT's 110 mile Houston Subdivision. This entire subdivision was rebuilt from 1975 to 1977 using a $19 million loan, acquired by way of a federal assistance program for ailing railroads. A second federally guaranteed loan for $12 million was used to upgrade large sections of the mainline between Durant, Oklahoma and Waco, Texas during 1977 and 1978. These improvements were necessary because of agreements entered into between the MKT and two separate power companies for the transport of low-sulfur western coal to two new on-line electric generating plants. The first plant was completed in 1978 by the Lower Colorado River Authority at LaGrange, Texas, on the Houston Subdivision, while the second plant was built by the Grand River Dam Authority at Prior, Oklahoma between 1978 and 1981. The huge LCRA plant at LaGrange required the continuous operation of four 110 car trains, with an estimated annual consumption of 20,000 cars of coal. *(John B. Charles)*

*(Bottom)* This ad appeared in *Railway Age* magazine in January 1978 and was one of the first advertisements placed by the conservative Whitman administration. Funding for promotional publications and advertising, as expended by the previous Barriger regime, was thought to have been frivolus by President R.N. Whitman in the early 1970's. Even the periodic publication of revised employee timetables was considered unnecessary and wasteful by Mr. Whitman, until it was finally deemed essential to issue System Timetable No. 1 in January 1975; this was the first new timetable distributed by the MKT since 1968! In order to control printing expenses for company publications, the Katy established its own print shop and bindery at Denison in the mid-70's. However, along with rising net revenues came a change in the MKT's policy toward advertising. By 1979, the advertising budget was expanded to also include expenses for costly radio advertisements, at least in the most populous market areas, and in 1982 the Katy began the annual publication of a twelve-page company calendar. *(R.B. George Collection)*

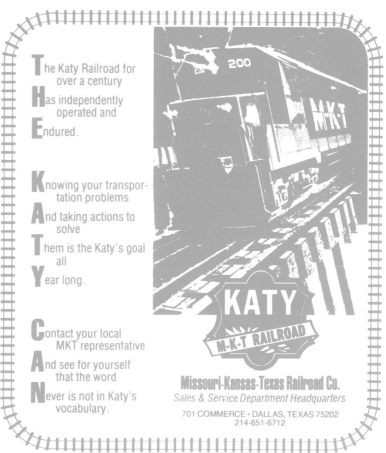

(*Above*) At Granger, Texas on the afternoon of October 12, 1977, No. 22, Amtrak's northbound INTER-AMERICAN, was running ahead of impending storm clouds. Both blades of Granger's train order semaphore were in the up position, indicating orders must be picked up by every train that passed the depot, north or southbound. Nos. 21 and 22 provided passenger service between St. Louis, Missouri and Laredo, Texas in the 1970's and was the predecessor of today's TEXAS EAGLE which operates between Chicago and San Antonio. In 1975 the Katy was awarded a contract by Amtrak for operation on the MKT's mainline between the stations of Temple and Taylor, Texas, which cut 40 miles from the INTER-AMERICAN'S former routing. Aided by federal funding, the work of upgrading Katy track conditions to handle passenger train speeds of up to 70 mph began September 2, 1975. Previous to his becoming president of the Katy Railroad, R.N. Whitman had served as Federal Railroad Administrator in 1969-1970 and supervised the establishment of government-operated passenger service, soon known as AMTRAK. (*Earl Holloway*)

(*Above*) In September 1978, the Katy accepted delivery of eleven 3000 horsepower EMD SD40-2 units, numbered 600-610. These and subsequent SD40-2s were the the only six-axle units owned by the Katy. Shown at Denison on October 11, 1978 is new #606 in regular freight service. One month later, the SD40-2s were placed in assigned service handling coal trains between Ft. Worth and the new LCRA power plant at LaGrange, Texas. The first coal train was delivered on November 28, 1978, which is possibly the most significant date in the history of the modern Katy Railroad and the administration of R.N. Whitman. (*Earl Holloway*)

(Above)   SD40-2s #615 and #618 were gleaming in the morning sunshine of November 3, 1979, as they hustled southbound  train No. 105 past the lovely old station at Temple, Texas.  These new engines were among eight units that arrived from EMD just two months earlier as the Katy's second order for heavy six-axle power.  Temple's station was constructed in 1912 by the M.K.&T. of Texas and is the only surviving example of Katy "mission style" architecture in the state of Texas.  The most prominent element of the design is the lofty tower that displays two enormous cast concrete Katy emblems and the words TEMPLE.  Fortunately, this building was donated to the city of Temple by the Union Pacific Railroad in 1992 for use as a library and archive for the city's new Railroad and Pioneer Museum.  *(Mike Bledsoe)*

(Below)   Westbound train No. 163, powered by lone GP38-2 #316, has reached the northern outskirts of Wichita Falls, Texas on Novmber 10, 1978.  At that time the Katy was providing tri-weekly service to Wichita Falls and the isolated Western Subdivision via 114 miles of trackage rights on the FW&D (Burlington Route) from Ft.Worth.  In 1980 the I.C.C. approved the MKT's application to abandon 64 miles of track between the Texas/Oklahoma state line and Altus, Oklahoma, subject to the purchase of the line by the state of Oklahoma.  By June 1984, sixty miles of track had been rebuilt north of the Red River with state funds in order to maintain service to Altus from Wichita Falls, with the MKT appointed as the contracted operator of the line by the state of Oklahoma.  *(Dr. Theron Baber)*

*(Opposite, above)* Four SD40-2s are unloading a 110-car coal train at the dumping station of the LCRA power plant near LaGrange, Texas in November 1980. The Katy delivered an 11,000-ton coal train to this plant approximately four times each week. *(Bruce Blalock)*

With the addition of coal train revenues to its already healthy marketing base, gross earnings for the MKT surged to $222 million in 1980. Surprisingly, the Katy registered a net income of only $1.7 million in 1980, primarily because of a huge increase in overall operating expenses of $32 million. Reduced income tax credits and an adjustment in a tax allocation agreement with the MKT's parent corporation, Katy Industries of Elgin, Illinois, also contributed to this performance.

*(Opposite, below)* At Gap, Oklahoma, GP-40 #205 was caught literally in mid-stream, crossing the scenic Limestone Creek viaduct with a southbound train in October 1980. This was one the most beautiful locations on the Katy, prior to the rebuilding and widening of U.S. Highway 69 in 1986-1988. A new highway bridge now obscures this view. *(Tom Balzen)*

*(Above)* Eastbound train No. 102 was found crossing Loutre Creek, near McKittrick, Missouri on the morning of October 7, 1981. McKittrick had been a fuel and water stop on the 189 mile St. Louis Subdivision during the Katy's steam era. Power for No. 102 was supplied by GP38-2 #311 and a leased black Conrail unit, #8152. *(Raymond George, Jr.)*

*(Left)* The Katy's business had improved to such an extent in the early 1980's that additional cabooses were leased from the Alaska Railroad. Alaska #1084 and Katy #131 were photographed in action near Taylor, Texas on January 2, 1981, *(Mike Bledsoe)*

(Left) Southbound train No. 101 was stretched out across the Missouri River bottoms as it crossed the Katy's impressive 1,638-foot bridge at Boonville, Missouri on a clear August morning in 1981. Leased Conrail GP38-2 #8220 and two freshly painted Katy GP-40s are gathering momentum for the climb up the 1.4% grade of Boonville Hill, which begins immediately south of the bridge. The most interesting feature of this bridge is a 408-foot long lift span, which was designed to be raised to accomodate river traffic. Three 300-foot fixed spans were erected north of the lift span, while a 247-foot fixed span and a 60-foot through plate girder were constructed south of the lift span. When the bridge was finished in 1932, the lift span was the longest such structure in the world. Prior to 1982, operators were on 24-hour duty between March and November to raise and lower the span for river traffic. An automatic interlocking system protected the approaches to the bridge from train movements while the lift span was up. During winter months, when the river was closed to navigation, the lift span was lowered for the season.

The Boonville Bridge was left high and dry when the MKT abandoned 200 miles of its St. Louis and Sedalia Subdivisions in 1987. Later that year the Katy sold the right-of-way to the state of Missouri for use as a hiking and biking trail; however, the huge bridge was not included in the deal. Since the 1988 UP/MKT merger, the bridge has belonged to the Union Pacific Railroad, which continues to serve Boonville by way of its ex-Missouri Pacific River Division. Like its massive lift span, the bridge's future is now in the air. (Raymond George, Jr.)

(Right) Among those special places visited by most diehard Katy buffs was the famous Rocheport tunnel, located on the St. Louis Subdivision, eleven miles east of the division point at Franklin, Missouri. Built in 1892-93, during the construction of the 189 mile St. Louis Subdivision, it had the distinction of being the only tunnel on the Katy Railroad. Changes came quickly when the MKT and Union Pacific made a trackage rights trade-off agreement in 1986 that gave the UP operating rights on the Katy's central Oklahoma corridor and allowed the Katy to use the UP's more direct route between Sedalia and St. Louis, Missouri. Applications for the abandonment of 200 miles of the Katy's own St. Louis Subdivision and a portion of its Sedalia Subdivision followed shortly afterwards. By March 22, 1986, when this photograph of eastbound No. 102 was snapped at Rocheport, operations on the St. Louis Subdivision were nearing their close. The MKT's new routing on the UP between Sedalia and St. Louis was inaugurated on April 14, 1986. The fate of the old St. Louis Subdivision was sealed when a devastating Missouri River flood struck in the autumn of 1986 that assured the I.C.C.'s approval of the applications for abandonment on March 6, 1987. By the end of 1987, rail and ties had been removed by contractors and negotiations had been finalized with the state of Missouri for the purchase the 200 mile route between St. Charles and Sedalia for a hiking and biking trail. Today, Rocheport is a designated access point on the hiking trail, officially named "The Katy Trail," and the old tunnel is a very popular attraction for thousands of visitors annually. (Craig Shaw)

# 1983-1988: MISS KATY & UNCLE PETE

A healthy working relationship had existed between the Union Pacific, affectionately nicknamed "Uncle Pete," and the MKT for many years. Building on this foundation in June 1975, the Whitman administration and the UP began the successful operation of pre-blocked trains through interchange at Kansas City, Missouri. In August that same year, Union Pacific President John Kenefick inspected the Katy system by rail at the invitation of Mr. Whitman and the two executives soon became close personal friends. In January 1979, R.N. Whitman was elected Chairman of the Katy's Board of Directors and Harold Gastler moved from the Operating Department to become President of the MKT. Serious talks between Chairman Whitman and John Kenefick concerning the purchase of the Katy by the Union Pacific began in the early 1980's, after the MKT had been awarded trackage rights on the UP to Omaha and Lincoln, Nebraska by the I.C.C. as a result of the Katy's vigorous protest in 1981 to the approved merger of the Missouri Pacific and Union Pacific systems. The first public announcement of the intended UP/MKT merger was made May 22, 1985, but the two roads remained separate until the takeover was implemented on August 12, 1988. Interestingly, a palace revolt of sorts occurred in 1986 when unnamed Katy executive officers attempted to equal or better the price offered by the Union Pacific; however, this effort did not materialize because Mr. Whitman was convinced merger with the UP was the best choice for the MKT.

*(Above)* In 1980 the MKT established a subsidiary Oklahoma, Kansas and Texas Railroad Company on a temporary basis to operate the bankrupt Rock Island's route between Dallas, Texas and Topeka, Kansas. The arrangement became permanent in 1982 when the state of Oklahoma, a rail user's corporation and the MKT joined together to purchase 630 miles of the former Rock Island from Dallas-Ft. Worth to Salina, Kansas. In 1987, its last full year operating the OKT, the Katy netted nearly $1.5 million in clear profits and set a standard of excellence in service to its customers that the Union Pacific is now contractually required to maintain. Here, northbound OKT No. 504 has stopped at Chickasha, Oklahoma to pick up 30 cars of crushed stone and two locomotives on June 18, 1983. *(Raymond George, Jr.)*

*(Left)* The OKT's "coonskin" herald first appeared on a Katy annual report in 1983, in combination with the Katy's emblem; it had been designed by the MKT's Engineering Department at Denison, Texas.

*(Above)* Northbound OKT Extra 310 was rolling through Wellington, Kansas at 20 mph on the afternoon of June 17, 1983 behind two Katy units and leased Conrail GP-38 #7996. During the 1983 wheat harvest, twenty-five four-axle Geeps were subleased from Conrail for use on the MKT/OKT system; such power was well suited for use on light density Katy branch lines where deferred maintenance was still the norm. Green and yellow #310 was among ten EMD GP38-2s purchased in January 1973 that were the first group of new power ordered by the Whitman administration; by 1976, eighteen GP38-2s had been purchased, numbered 304-321. In addition to Katy's acquisition of new and leased power, increased operations on the OKT in 1983 warranted the purchase of eighteen ex-Conrail GP-40's, all built in 1968 for the Penn Central. Ex-Conrail #3105-3112, 3114, 3116, 3120, 3122, 3133, 3139, 3144, 3152, 3161 and 3167 were renumbered MKT #231-248. The MKT painted its ex-Conrail engines in the green and yellow livery as individual units required major servicing at the Parsons shops. However, after the 1985 announcement of the intended merger of the MKT and UP, the repainting program for ex-Conrail and other second-hand power was suspended, with only a hastily stenciled "M-K-T" placed over the former owner's paint scheme. *(Raymond George, Jr.)*

*(Left)* Behind two big SD40-2s and a GP-40, a southbound Katy grain extra was departing the Union Pacific's Council Bluffs, Iowa yard on July 27, 1985. In January 1983, the MKT excercised its rights granted by the I.C.C. as a condition of the UP/MP merger to operate north of Kansas City on the UP's Omaha Subdivision to reach Lincoln and Omaha, Nebraska and the Council Bluffs yards. Business for the Katy on the northern extension was initially very heavy. During the 1983 harvest, as many as three Katy trains were in daily operation between Kansas City and Omaha, causing upper level UP management to take a much closer look at this lean little competitor. The combination of OKT and northern extension mileage increased the Katy system to 3,099 miles and helped account for a rise in gross income to $250.5 million in 1983. *(Charles D. Hunter)*

*(Above)* Westbound Katy No. 101 was descending the elevated tracks fronting the Mississippi River at St. Louis, Missouri on October 12, 1985; in the background is the majestic Gateway Arch and Busch Stadium, home of the 1985 National League Champion St. Louis Cardinals baseball team. Prior to the 1980's, St. Louis train spotters rarely saw Katy activity because the MKT's Baden Yard was remotely located in the northern suburbs of the Mound City. On this date, No. 101 was detouring over the rails of the St. Louis Terminal Railroad Association in order to reach the Union Pacific mainline that would be used for the 227 mile trip west to the Katy connection at Sedalia, Missouri. This scene became more familiar to local railfans after April 14, 1986, when Katy trains began using trackage rights over this same route on a permanent basis.

*(Below)* On March 22, 1986, eastbound No. 102 was passing the open train order station at North Jefferson, Missouri on its route to St. Louis. This was one of the last trains to use the Katy's old St. Louis Subdivision, prior to the shift of operations to trackage rights on the UP between Sedalia and St. Louis the following month. The pictured right-of-way is now a section of Missouri's 200 mile "Katy Trail" for hikers and bicyclists. Directly behind lead GP38-2 #318 was #387, one of nine secondhand GP39-2s purchased from the Kennecott Copper Corporation late in 1984. Ex-KCC #779-783, 785 and 787-789 were renumbered MKT #380-388. Other purchases of "used" power involved nineteen GP-38s that were formerly owned by the Illinois Central Gulf Railroad. Ex-ICG #9500-9509 and 9511-9519 were renumbered MKT #325-343. *(Both- Craig Shaw)*

(Left, top) The skyline of Kansas City, Missouri takes a back seat to southbound No. 103, as it departs the Katy's Glen Park Yard on the afternoon of May 1, 1986. Leading the power lineup is GP-40 #234, formerly Conrail #3108, built by EMD in August 1968 and acquired by the Katy in 1983. Three additional ex-Conrail GP-38s, originally numbered 7795, 7801 and 7813, completed the list of Katy-owned second-hand power; these units received MKT numbers 322-324. (Scott Muskopf)

During 1986, system car loads decreased slightly by 1.2%; however, unit train coal was down drastically by 24.6% because on-line power plants had begun using low priced natural gas to supplement coal usage. These figures helped the Union Pacific in its arguments before the Interstate Commerce Commission that the Katy was a "failing-firm," even though the MKT earned a net income of $22.8 million in 1986. The MKT's own argument for the merger with UP stated that although the Katy was currently earning income, "its future in a deregulated, post-Staggers Act environment was not good."

(Left, bottom) Two seemingly ageless GP-7s were teamed up for the yard job at Bellmead, Texas on the afternoon of July 2, 1987. Hign-nosed #109 and #115 were among only six GP-7s that had not been modified with lowered short hoods by that date. Although the MKT's thirty-three GP-7s were in overall excellent condition, the Union Pacific chose to sell the entire group shortly after the takeover and many are still in service on various shortlines today. Visible in the background is the power house stack and main erection bay of the Katy's vacant Warden Locomotive Shops that had been in service from 1923 to 1958. In 1980, the MKT constructed additional track and installed a high speed fueling station at Bellmead Yard to avoid delays to expedited trains at the more congested Ft. Worth and Denison engine facilities. (David Fasules)

(Opposite, above) From a lofty perch, on March 26, 1988, photographer Daniel Schroeder found eastbound Katy No. 102 on the western outskirts of St. Louis, at Pacific, Missouri, utilizing trackage rights over the Union Pacific. This "bird's eye view" also shows the close proximity of rival Burlington Northern's trackage, which is literally at the water's edge of the unpredictable Meramec River. Directly behind lead GP-40 #234 is slave unit #401B, the only such unit on the Katy's roster. In 1974, Parsons Shop Superintendent Paul Larery supervised the redesign of ex-F3A #66C (originally #203C when built in 1947) to an F38M. Independent controls were removed from the cab and the windows were blanked out, in addition to building a doorway into the nose. The unit was originally numbered 399B and renumbered 401B in 1975. This oddity did not fit into the Union Pacific's plans after the August takeover and was donated to the city of Denison in 1989, where it is currently displayed at the Red River Railroad Museum.

(Opposite, below) Northbound No. 142, appropriately nicknamed "The Salty," was crossing the spectacular Galveston Causeway Bridge on July 2, 1988. Among the Katy's most interesting, yet rarely photographed, assigned turnaround runs was that of Nos. 141 and 142, which operated on the jointly-owned Galveston, Houston & Henderson Railroad between Houston and the island city of Galveston, Texas. Since the days of the notorious Jay Gould, the MKT and the Missouri Pacific shared equally in the ownership of the 50 mile GH&H and this arrangement remained unchanged after the UP/MP merger in 1981. "The Salty's" power lashup on that day was pure mid-80's Katy, led by GP-40s #227 and #226, separated by road slug #501. This threesome operated systemwide as a single unit that was never parted, except for heavy maintenance, and had been christened "The Three Stooges" by train crews. Never known to waste anything, the MKT's mechanical department had built road slug #501 from wrecked GP-40 #222 in 1982 at the Parsons shops. Also providing power for "The Salty" was an additional unknown GP-40 and one of the nineteen ugly, yet well-liked, ex-Illinois Central Gulf GP-38s. (John B. Charles)

*(Above)* This was classic KATY at its best! The rear brakeman has snagged his set of flimsies from the train order stand as caboose #127 of this southbound train whipped by the Durant, Oklahoma depot at 50 mph on June 8, 1986. In the siding, waiting for clearance from the Durant operator, was lead unit #630 of the northbound HCX ("Houston-Chicago Express"), which was operated daily in combination with the Milwaukee Road via the connection at Kansas City. Following the 1988 UP-MKT merger, the old joint Frisco-Katy station at Durant was closed and later demolished by the Union Pacific. SD40-2 #630 is now sporting the UP's yellow, red and gray livery and has been renumbered 3837. Lastly, caboose #127 escaped the cutting torch and was donated to the city of New Franklin, Missouri for display by the Union Pacific in 1991; it now wears its original red paint scheme and insignia dating from 1968. *(Raymond George, Jr.)*

*As described on the preceding pages, the MKT became adept at surviving at a subsistence level for over a decade, prior to its recovery. Without doubt, the Katy's greatest asset was its dedicated employees, both union and non-union, who struggled monumentally to help the company exist from day to day during the hardest times. Even though the MKT had been openly groomed for merger over a period of twenty years, most employees and friends of the Katy found it difficult to witness this proud road's voluntary demise in 1988, after 118 years of continuous service. On the verge of bankruptcy in 1964, company earnings and train operations were at their highest levels at the time of the merger with Union Pacific. The Katy's history thus ended quietly, if not heroically, with apologies offered to none.*

*– Raymond B. George, Jr.*
*April 25, 1993*